After Lives

VERSO

180 Varick Street
New York, NY 10014-4606

Telephone
(212) 807-9680

Fax
(212) 807-9152

(distributed by Routledge)

Title:

After Lives

Author:

Barbara Harlow

Publication date:

January 30, 1997

Price:

$17.00; paperback original

Contact:

Laura Secor

We would appreciate receiving two copies of your review.
Thank you.

After Lives

Legacies of
Revolutionary Writing

◆

BARBARA HARLOW

VERSO
London • New York

First published by Verso 1996
© Barbara Harlow 1996
All rights reserved

Verso
UK: 6 Meard Street, London W1V 3HR
USA: 180 Varick Street, New York NY 10014–4606

Verso is the imprint of New Left Books

ISBN 1–85984–825–7
ISBN 1–85984–180–5 (pbk)

British Library Cataloguing in Publication Data
A catalogue record for this book is available from the British Library

Library of Congress Cataloging-in-Publication Data
A catalog record for this book is available from the Library of Congress

Typeset by M Rules
Printed and bound in Great Britain by
Biddles Ltd, Guildford and King's Lynn

for Katie and Ryan and Sean

Contents

Acknowledgements

When I first began to learn of and from the writings of Ghassan Kanafani, Roque Dalton and Ruth First, each of them had already been assassinated, but their deaths were still immediately remembered by close friends and distant admirers alike. That was still in the time, so to speak, of "resistance literature." Now, more than a decade later, their works – and the resistance movements – for and with which they struggled in Palestine, in El Salvador and in South Africa have entered into an era and an arena of dramatic and compelling changes and challenges, with new sets of terms and issues: from the duresses of interrogation, to the controversies of negotiation and eventually the contradictions of electoral participation and the complexities of state formation. This project too, *After Lives: Legacies of Revolutionary Writing*, in its own considerably lesser way, has been, even if differently, cumulatively informed over the last decade and a half by some of those same transformations in the arenas of cultural politics and international relations. My own background over the last three decades in the traditions of literary criticism, from the "new criticism" to more current theoretical trends, has in its own way no doubt influenced the approach to – and focus on – the written works of the writers who were martyred for their revolutionary activity. It is to be hoped, however, that those same literary critical traditions are able to respond to the ongoing pressures of historical circumstance and current events, and to the combined exigencies of theorizing modes and more empirical imperatives – the proverbial contest between academia and activism. However, these essays are neither straightforward bio-graphy, nor a political history of liberation struggle in the years of decolonization; rather they seek to inquire into the critical questions of life and death that the examples of Kanafani, Dalton and First proposed through their own writing, and that they continue to pose in the many and varied posthumous readings of their work.

While the political assassination of writers loomed illicitly large over the lives and work of the revolutionaries discussed in the following pages, it is now the legalized death penalty that threatens as decisively the challenges to change. Over the course of the summer of 1995, during which some of these pages were revisited and revised, Mumia Abu-Jamal – journalist, former Black Panther, writer, and political prisoner – waited still on death row (where he had been held for more than a decade), but by then with an impending execution date. On 1 June 1995, Pennsylvania governor Tom Ridge had signed his death warrant for 17 August. Just over two months later, however, following an international campaign on his behalf and against the death penalty, Abu-Jamal was granted an indefinite stay of execution, in order to prepare his appeal for a hearing for a new trial. Could it be that campaigns can still be mobilized – and to some effect? That there are, after all, continuing terrains of struggle? Months later, the appeals on Abu-Jamal's behalf were still in process and, on another continent, on 10 November 1995, the Abacha-led government in Nigeria had, despite international protest, executed the writer Ken Saro-Wiwa and eight of his col-leagues. Accused of treachery against the state, the men had been actively opposing the combined designs on Ogoniland in Nigeria by the Nigerian government and Shell British-Petroleum. Further protests against the executions followed, including calls for embargos, economic sanctions and boycotts, and involved par-ticipating nations of the Commonwealth conference, Organization for African Unity, South African president Nelson Mandela, even members of the United States Congress and the Royal Geographical Society, as well as human rights organiza-tions and concerned supporters. Meanwhile, at Fort Benning, Georgia, the US Army's School of the Americas continued its infamous intercontinental training programs in "counter-insurgency."

In the meantime, there are many people and organizations that I want to acknowledge and thank for supporting my own interrupted work on this project. I can mention by name here only a few: Chris Maziar who helped engineer revisits to El Salvador and the Occupied Territories (and cyberspace), Hatem Natsheh who was always ready with resources of commentary and translation, Ruth Wilson Gilmore and Craig Gilmore who provoked the first part on assassination and have been friends ever since. Mary Benson and Ronald Segal were enormously helpful in arranging the opportunity to consult significant portions of Ruth First's papers that are held at the Institute of Commonwealth Studies in London, where David Blake and his colleagues provided excellent support. Nels Johnson and Sarah Graham-Brown were splendid too in their discussions of each day's readings. The hospitality of friends at Birzeit University in Ramallah and the Alternative Informative Center in West Jerusalem, Barbara Buntman and her family (Johnny, Fran, Daniel and Ari – as well as Manuel Orozco) in South Africa, and CISPES and other colleagues in El Salvador, must also be gratefully acknowledged and much thanked. Michael Sprinker was an inspiring editor. And Jane Hindle, Valerie Mendes, Ruth Petrie and others at Verso have provided wonderful comment and support. Finally, Nimr, Grainne and Ibtisam helped in their own particular ways with much of the work of composition and word processing.

Preface

The essays collected in *After Lives: Legacies of Revolutionary Writing* propose a critical reading of a contemporary cultural politics that has been historically invested in the various practices of interrogation, assassination and negotiation. The essays' combined focus is centered around three intellectuals – Ghassan Kanafani, Popular Front for the Liberation of Palestine (PFLP), Roque Dalton, Ejercito Revolucionario del Pueblo (ERP), El Salvador and Ruth First, South African Communist Party (SACP) and African National Congress (ANC). All three were victims of the first two of these practices and in their writing each anticipated the latter.

The readings of Kanafani, Dalton and First, three major contributors to the elaboration of strategies and theories of resistance at the acme of national liberation struggles, are at once historically closured and critically re-articulated by the dramatically transformed states of political affairs out of which the writers emerged and to which they contributed in the crucial decades of the 1950s, 1960s, and 1970s. In South Africa, for example, the ANC and SACP, unbanned in 1990, engaged in negotiations with the apartheid government to end apartheid rule; and in May 1994, in the first free elections ever in that country, Nelson Mandela was elected as the nation's president. While the new government was established to represent the larger spectrum of South African politics, it was significantly made up of former ANC members, many of whom, like

Mandela, had spent long years in prison. In the meantime, a hemisphere away, the Farabundo Martí National Liberation Front (FMLN), the combined successor in El Salvador to the ERP and its parallel organizations, following its meetings in Mexico with Salvadoran government representatives, and the signing of the Peace Accords on 16 January 1992 in Chapultepec, Mexico, similarly contested elections in April 1994. Less successful than the ANC, the FMLN nonetheless secured a position for itself in El Salvador's new parliament as well as in many municipalities – only to split once again, in early 1995, over the issue of the proper critical role for the historical resistance in the political processes of the post-election period. Finally, in "Palestine," the intifada, or Palestinian uprising, itself a translation of traditional Palestine Liberation Organization (PLO) structures from "outside" to "inside," or from out of exile to under occupation, underwent a strategic re-evaluation of its sociopolitical agenda in the aftermath of the 1990–91 Gulf War, just as Palestinian representatives were demanding full status as a negotiating delegation in its own right at the conference table. That demand, however, would be usurped by the Gaza Jericho First Agreement, signed by Yasser Arafat and Yitzhak Rabin in September 1993, and the subsequent establishment of a "Palestinian Authority" in those limited two areas. Arafat's organization would seem to have taken over from the Israelis the charge of policing the intifada. With these examples before it, then, and in still another political space, the Sinn Fein/IRA leadership considered – often against popular concerns for more consultation and/or less compromise – the demand from Downing Street that they decommission arms in order to secure even a precarious place at Britain's negotiating table. "Democracy" and "negotiation," in other words – and together with such attendant terms as "elections," "policing," "transitions" – have, in the 1990s, in a most important sense displaced (albeit still controversially) "armed struggle" as the focal point of cultural and political debate.

The sketches that follow, then, are neither straightforward biography nor exhaustive historiography, but represent an attempt to inquire into the reciprocal effects of popular struggle and individual life narratives and their respective critical contributions to current assessments of the place and dynamic of political dissent and theoretical debate. The look back is seeking the ways in which these intellectuals looked ahead (even as they failed, as some would maintain, to "watch their backs"). "Writers, martyrs, revolutionaries": Kanfani, Dalton and First were all of these, although not necessarily in that order. Their writings continue to be read and discussed; they were assassinated by their enemies, but perhaps it was their followers who made martyrs of them; as revolutionaries, their example remains as part of their "after lives." What might be the apparent anachronicities of the title are part of their critical example. As Jorge Semprun (1975, p. 1) maintained in his introduction to Fernando Claudin's history of the Communist Movement and referring to its author who had been expelled from the Spanish Communist Party, "[a]ctually, one is always expelled at the wrong moment, either too late or too soon". So too with assassination, perhaps, as with expulsion and thus, rather than solving the questions of their deaths, providing, in other words, the answers to the "whodunits" of the murders, these essays propose that it is precisely in their construction of, and participation in, question and answer periods – from interrogation to negotiation – and their different discursive formats that Kanafani, Dalton and First left important critical marks.

The organization of this study around disparate versions of "intellectual biography" suggests, however, an additional analysis which would also emphasize the relation of a writer not only to their work, but also to the social and political order within which they live and write – and die. The combined task of both "exhuming corpses" and "examining corpuses" also seeks to allow for a discussion of the complex, often conflicted, position of the intellectual within the structures of a political party and/or organized resistance movement: Ghassan Kanafani and the PFLP, Roque Dalton and the ERP, and Ruth First and the SACP/ANC. The fact that each of these intellectuals was assassinated also raises – and perhaps even more urgently now – the question of the political consequentiality of cultural work and the historical responsibility of the critic – on both sides of the revolution. According to Margaret Keck (1995, p. 39) for example, in her "typology of activism," the new, if disputed, difference between "solidarity" and human rights work is that between the "risk-sharing" of the former and the task of information gathering and verification of the latter:

> The solidarity and rights frameworks have been two of the main patterns on which international advocacy has taken place among non-governmental organizations. Although both involve relationships between oppressed peoples and those in a position to support them, there are important conceptual differences. Individuals are endowed with rights; communities are the repositories of solidarity. Solidarity involves a substantive dimension that rights-based activism does not: support based on a conviction that those supported are right. Human rights appeals, on the other hand, raise procedural claims: that violations of personhood or of accepted civil or legal norms and procedures are unacceptable regardless of the victim's beliefs.

In the three central essays that follow, the work of three intellectuals is considered, particularly the engagement of each in questions of both solidarity and rights, of individuals and of peoples, and of risks no less than procedures. Included in appendices are brief bio-bibliographical sketches of each of the writers, with information on their main published works. Indeed, it is on such work – rather than biographic or ethnographic research – that these essays depend. Other works – critical, historical, referential – cited in the text are identified in a bibliography at the end of the book.

"The politics of terminations": Ghassan Kanafani's first novel, *Men in the Sun* (1961), was remade as a film that radically altered the text's ending. The issue of endings, as their identified terminations reappear in the last years of the writer's life, years of crisis for the Palestinian resistance from 1970 to 1972, are investigated in a series of articles that he wrote for *al-Hadaf* (the newspaper that Kanafani both founded and edited until his death) and in *Shu'un Filastiniya* (published by the PLO Research Center in Beirut, an institution whose premises were ransacked and archives confiscated by the Israeli army when it invaded Lebanon in 1982).

"The politics of amnesty": in the case of Roque Dalton, the

circumstances and consequences of his death have for twenty years now been the subject of both debate and doubt, and the objects of the many rewritings of his story. To forgive or to forget? Amnesty or amnesia? *Habeas corpus* – Who has the body? But Dalton was committed to debate and his engagement with it is the focus of readings here of two of his books: the *testimonio*, *Miguel Marmol*, and the protracted exchange on the prospects of the future of the left in Latin America, *¿Revolución en la revolución? y la crítica de derecha*.

And "the politics of dissent": it is, in turn, Ruth First's extended bibliography that differently organizes the trajectory of the third of these essays, "After the Fact." As journalist and historian, First challenged the ascendant chronologies and maps of domination, in Africa in particular, but appealing as well to other agendas of continental struggle and visions of intersecting international and national liberations.

Those chronologies are suggested in the opening chapter, "Writers and Assassinations," and its brief accounts of a fellowship of martyred writers. They are revisited again in the concluding essay, "New Geographies of Struggle," that seeks latterly to recapitulate the concatenations of some of the new as well as renewed exigencies of writing and criticism in what has been called the "post-bi-polar world order" (see Landsberg, 1994), from interrogation and assassination to negotiation, from the death penalty to truth commissions. As the Irish sociologist, Mike Tomlinson, has elsewhere proposed (1995, p. 17), the concern that remains is precisely the "problem of how wars end and what to do with the peace."

Kanafani, Dalton and First were unrelenting in their lives and work as critics of their own commitments to revolutionary change. According to Kanafani, for example, the ideal of a "democratic secular state" in Palestine was a mere theoretical delusion betrayed if it could not be articulated and consolidated through the practices of a "democratic revolution." And Dalton, in his own turn, always demanded, as he had insisted once in his 1963 essay, "Poetry and Militancy in Latin America," that the recognition must always be that the "matter is not so simple" (p. 14). First also continues to be remembered for her "sharp tongue." She differed strongly, at times adamantly, with her colleagues on many issues: from Hungary in 1956 and Afghanistan in the early 1980s, China versus the Soviet Union, to the rights of the Eritrean people to struggle for their self-determination. As Shawn Slovo would remember of her parents, Ruth First and Joe Slovo, who often conflicted dramatically on several such issues: "You could set them off really. [We (Shawn and her sisters, Gillian and Robyn) used to] do it actually, at Christmas and times when we were together here. And we'd just throw in some kind of remark about Russia, or some remark about China, because Ruth was pro-China. And they'd just go at it" (interview with Buntman).

Ghassan Kanafani, Roque Dalton and Ruth First, committed critics each, and at a time when criticism and commitment often challenged the other's practices, in their own work, as in their persistent example, continue to give critical dissent a good name. And now again, perhaps, that dissent, those names – their names – might well discover re-examined terrains of debate and renewed histories of the future. Might their radical visions keep them potentially under threat of death in the current era of "democracy" and "negotiation?" What, in other words, would they say now?

PART I

WRITERS AND ASSASSINATIONS

You do not die because you are created or because you have a body.
You die because you are the face of the future.
Adonis, "The Desert" (1982)

People who die for the freedom of others are, like women who die in childbirth, difficult to explain except to those for whom they died.
Fawaz Turki, *Soul in Exile* (1988)

Everyone has the right to life, liberty and security of person.
Article 3: Universal Declaration of Human Rights (1948)

On 22 July 1987, the Palestinian cartoonist Naji al-Ali was shot on a London street outside the offices of *al-Qabas*, a Kuwaiti newspaper for which at the time he drew his political caricatures. On 29 August 1987, some six weeks later, Naji al-Ali died from those wounds, without regaining consciousness. His last cartoon, drawn just before his assassination, was strangely ominous. In it, Hanzalla, the "child of the camps" who appeared in all his drawings, standing with his back to the viewer, observing the corruption, exploitation and repression in and of the Arab world that Naji al-Ali's cartoons relentlessly depicted, lay now face down on the ground, an arrow in his heel, killed perhaps by the same forces of political oppression that for the last decade and a half the cartoonist had committed himself to exposing.

In the immediate aftermath of the shooting – the assailant has still, and amid continued rumor and speculation, gone unapprehended – writers, critics, ideologues and friends of the Arab artist raised collectively and in individual articles the insistent question: Who killed Naji al-Ali? Univocal as the question might have been, the proffered answers, some tentative, others accusatory, were decidedly dissonant. The *Observer*, in London, on the day following the artist's death, blamed the PLO. Reporting a phone call that Naji al-Ali had allegedly received from Yasser Arafat's organization warning him to "correct his attitude," the *Observer* article went on to describe Naji al-Ali's subsequent cartoon critiquing the Palestinian resistance and its leadership. It concluded from these details that "the tone may have cost him his life".

Various factions within the PLO, including Yasser Arafat's Fatah, Iran, the Palestinian renegade-extremist Abu Nidal, and Mossad, the Israeli secret service, were variously accused in the months that followed of assassinating the Arab world's most popular and well-known cartoonist. An editorial in the 14 September 1987 issue of *al-Hadaf*, the weekly magazine of the Popular Front for the Liberation of Palestine (PFLP), however, asked further – and with implications for that other, more preliminary question of "who killed Naji al-Ali?" – "Why was Naji al-Ali buried in London?" Why in London and not in Palestine where he was born, or in Ain al-Hilweh, the Palestinian refugee camp in southern Lebanon where he had grown up? Two answers were suggested by the editorial. The first explanation invoked reasons of security: given the cartoonist's reputation and renown and the popular anger at his death, could state security forces contain, or even predict, the force of people's reactions to the loss of this exemplar? The second response was more provocative still: Naji al-Ali's burial in London testified to his controversial independence, his contentious and critical ideological positioning *vis-à-vis* the Arab regimes, and his insistent "representation" of all the Arab peoples who, like the Palestinians, are systematically exploited by those same concupiscent regimes. Issues of nationalism presaged, even then, the encomiums of another internationalism still to be determined.

In a commemorative poem, one Palestinian poet, Murid Barghuti, seconded this indictment of the Arab regimes and their reactionary politics when, in an allusion to the biblical Joseph story, he suggested that it was not the wolf at all who had killed Joseph but his own brothers. For Mahmud Darwish, another Palestinian poet and then head of the General Union of Palestinian Writers, Naji al-Ali's assassination was the occasion to scrutinize the current political and cultural discourse of much of the Arab world. In an article in *al-Yawm al-Sabia* on 3 August 1987 entitled "No to Assassination by Bullets, No to Assassination with Words," Darwish wrote that "for every bullet there is more than one killer and more than one victim." Much as Israel has sought the mass removal and territorial and political dispossession of the Palestinian people, whether by assassination or transportation, and now "ghettoization", so too, according to Darwish, had "assassination come to characterize the dialogue of the Arabs with themselves."

What was it that had singled out Naji al-Ali for death by an assassin's bullet and assigned him a place in the pantheon of martyred artists? For Faysal Darraj, Radwa Ashur and Murid Barghuti in an article in the 17 August 1987 issue of *al-Hadaf*, "The Tragedy and the Greatness of the Different Artist," Naji al-Ali had distinguished himself by his very difference, his refusal to accept the dogma of doctrine either aesthetic or political. It was this tenacious independence that rendered the artist unacceptable, intolerable even, to regimes and systems that must, for their own self-preservation, suppress external opposition and contain internal contradiction. As an artist, the critics maintained, Naji al-Ali eschewed the structures of power as sanction for his work and chose instead, in order to transform the existing distorted relations of power, to draw from out of the arena of popular struggle. His political practice too differed from that of the politicians themselves in that he scorned the machinating maneuvers of opportunistic tactics, calculations, brokering and bargaining. Naji al-Ali's concerns and priorities were elsewhere. But where? What is the task of the political artist/the artist politician? And why should it get them killed?

In April 1988 in Mozambique, Albie Sachs did not die, despite the car bomb that sought to kill him. Sachs, a South African lawyer who had been imprisoned in 1963 under the 90 Day Detention Law, had on his release gone into exile in London and then Maputo. Currently serving as a Justice on South Africa's Constitutional Court, he has recounted the project of reconstruction – personal as well as political – that followed that assault on his person. In his memoir entitled *The Soft Vengeance of a Freedom Fighter* (1990c), both the body and the body politic are at stake in the writing. The scars left by the bomb blast are manifold: the loss of an arm and an eye, and the critical trauma no less to the rest of the corpus. In his memoir Sachs translates these traditional corporeal marks of physical violence into an anticipation of political reconstitution:

> This is a strange time to think that the struggle has become less simple, less direct, when I have just been a victim of an old-fashioned assassination attempt. Yet I feel convinced that one of the biggest tasks facing our movement at the moment is to overcome the psychology of the embattled and begin to think with the vision of leaders of the country as a whole. And yet, and yet, for all our new thinking, and breaking out of stereotypes, the police forces of the world continue their time-honoured surveillance and controls, and maybe I am just being naïve. (1990c, pp. 57–8)

For Sachs, "At least one's body is a whole entity, not fragmented into a million egos and currents and contradictory trends like political movements" (p. 173). The body and the body politic, the significance of assassination and its assessments notwithstanding, Sachs survived that attempt on his life. For those writers who did not, who were assassinated, the combined issues of exhuming the corpse and examining the corpus weigh heavy on their legacy to the "political movements" and their adherents.

Citing nationalism's political and cultural sway, its "imagined community" over the last two centuries, Benedict Anderson (1991, p. 7) has suggested that that very "fraternity" of national identification has made it possible "for so many millions of people, not so much to kill, as willingly to die for such limited imaginings". John D. Kelly (1995, p. 477) has gone on otherwise, in an examination of the "politics of shed blood," to question the connections between "the kind of blood you are born with" and the "kind of blood you shed", suggesting further that it "is not the abundance of martyrs but the value of stories of martyrs that is truly central here." "Martyrdom stories," he argues, "signal an effort to force a social alignment, to force a decision about a social truth" (pp. 488–9). Writers and their assassinations, in other words, engage precisely such a "politics of shed blood," but, just as significantly, the very stories of their life and work have dissented from, even militated against, the hagiographies of martyrology and/or opportunistic rehabilitations. In the stead of such eulogies, the writers had worked on behalf of critical re-readings. Had they lived, their stories would not only have turned out differently, but perhaps been written in another register as well.

During the two trips to Africa made in the last year of his life, and following his controversial departure from the ranks of Elijah Muhammad's Nation of Islam, Malcolm X sought support from the African heads of state that he had met with for his proposal to bring the historical situation of African Americans in the United States before the United Nations. That situation, like those of their counterparts in South Africa and Rhodesia, he argued at the time, should be globally condemned as a flagrant and wilful abuse of international covenants and agreements respecting the human rights of all peoples of the world. Malcolm X's work in Africa, like his activities in the United States, was meanwhile of considerable concern to the FBI who included in their copious files on him a *New York Times* article written from Cairo and dated 14 July 1964. It reported: "Malcolm X the black nationalist leader said today that he had come to attend a meeting of the council of ministers of the Organization of African Unity as an observer. He arrived yesterday. He said he intended to acquaint African heads of state 'with the true plight of America's Negroes and thus show them how our situation is as much a violation of the United Nations human rights charter as the situation in Africa and Mongolia'" (cited in Carson, 1991, p. 330). Malcolm X would, however, speak more challengingly – and decisively – to the same issue of international accountability on his return to the United States. In an interview on 2 December 1964 with radio talk-show host Les Crane, he asserted that: "[i]t's not a Negro problem or an American problem any longer. It's a world problem, it's a human problem. And so we're striving to lift it from the level of civil rights to the level of human rights. And at that level it's international. We can bring it into the United Nations and discuss it in the same tone and in the same language as the problems of people in other parts of the world also is [sic] discussed" (Malcolm X, 1989, p. 89). A few months later, just five days before he was assassinated in Harlem's Audubon Ballroom, Malcolm X returned to that transformative work that would link "civil rights" with "human rights" and make the United States internationally accountable for those rights. He had concluded his Rochester speech of 16 February 1965 with the provocative admonition:

> All nations that signed the charter of the UN came up with the Declaration of Human Rights and anyone who classifies his grievances under the label of "human rights" violations, those grievances can then be brought into the United Nations and be discussed by people all over the world. For as long as you call it "civil rights" your only allies can be the people in the next community, many of whom are responsible for your grievance. But when you call it "human rights" it becomes international. And then you can take your troubles to the World Court. You can take them before the world. And anybody anywhere on this earth can become your ally. (Malcolm X, 1989, p. 181)

Five days later, Malcolm X's body, as he rose to address a meeting of his newly formed Organization of Afro–American Unity, was riddled by assassins' bullets that did succeed, temporarily at least, in halting the international inquiry that the black leader had sought to initiate.

Much as the assassins had shot down the man – and a quarter of a century later, it is still in dispute who and how many they were, and at whose behest(s) they had carried out the attack – so the United States Congress, for a decade and a half, engaged in obstructing the project of bringing to bear in that country the various United Nation Covenants on human rights. While the United States, with most other UN member nations, had been among the signatories to the international organization's several charters, the Congress had (and in most cases has) yet to ratify those declarations and treaties. Of particular concern to congressional representatives at the time was the Genocide Convention, the first such treaty to be forwarded to the Senate for approval. Though the congressional objections, as Natalie Kaufman (1990) has pointed out, were largely indicative of subsequent opposition to the other treaties as well – they would "diminish basic rights," "promote world government," "enhance Soviet/Communist influence," "subject citizens to trial abroad," and "threaten the US form of government" – Senator

H. Alexander Smith (R.-N. J.) voiced the concerns of others in suggesting that genocide might well be worth killing for. According to Smith, referring, as did others who endorsed a similar position, to the history of African Americans, ratification of the Genocide Convention could mean that "[w]e may be charged with [genocide], that is the danger, and the Court of International Justice may say that there is a *prima facie* case made against the United States of genocide, and there you are, left, condemned in the eyes of the world" (cited in Kaufman, 1990, p. 45). That condemnation is precisely what Malcolm X, in linking the issues of "civil rights" with the imperatives of "human rights," was preparing to do when he was killed on 21 February 1965 by the assassins' desperate bullets.

Many questions have been raised over the last quarter of a century about the circumstances of Malcolm X's death. For Malik Miah, writing in 1976, in the introduction to *The Assassination of Malcolm X*, "Identifying the killers of Malcolm X, Martin Luther King, and Fred Hampton is not just a matter of historical interest. It is an urgent defensive measure for the Black movement, to prevent future assassinations of its leaders" (p. 12). Bruce Perry (1991) more cynically considers that "Revolutionaries are not required to succeed. Usually, they end up defeated or dead, martyrs to their chosen cause" (p. 280). For the FBI, the matter was different again. In a memorandum from 25 February 1965, the Bureau wrote:

MALCOLM K. LITTLE
INTERNAL SECURITY – MMI
In view of the subject's death, his name is being removed from the Security Index at the Bureau and you should handle accordingly in your office.

Submit an appropriate memorandum noting his death, for dissemination at the Bureau.

Attention [BUREAU DELETION].

Cancel SI cards (Cited in Carson, 1991, p. 383).

The question, however, of who killed Malcolm X, like the inquiries two decades later on another continent into the death of Naji al-Ali, is more than a defensive one, a cynical comment, or a "security index" card. It is a systemic question, a historical one. What happens should genocide turn to assassination?

The very function of the author, at least in Western culture, according to Michel Foucault in "What Is an Author?", is to "limit, exclude, choose." The author's putative self, in other words, provides the "functional principle by which, in our culture . . . one impedes the free circulation, the free manipulation, the free composition, decomposition and recomposition of fiction" (Foucault, 1979, p. 159). The author, Foucault maintains, is "the ideological figure by which one marks the manner in which we fear the proliferation of meaning" (p. 159). The critical convention governing the concept of "author" presupposes the separation of the artist from the political conditions within which they write, the ideological milieu within which they work. Such a separation between a self and an other, the rhetorical basis of a politics of identity, itself crucial to the definition of author as Foucault presents it, is a cordon that Naji al-Ali, for example, refutes, that his drawings confute. The collapse of the inherited distinction between culture and politics is, however, anathema to the dominant structures of power which continue to insist on what Terry Eagleton (1990, p. 33) has called the "stalest of Arnoldian clichés, [that] the 'poetic' as we have it today was, among other things, historically constructed to carry out just that business of suppressing political conflict." The guardians of cultural preserves and political dominion must maintain the separation of culture and politics at least in so far as this separation underwrites their territorial elitism and the ideological mystification whereby such ascendancy remains unassailed. The politicians must, for their part, be wary lest something called "culture" be wrested from the control of their servitors, whom they have appointed and whose services the state apparatus has again and again enlisted, and begin to function in mobilizing popular political opposition. The language of objectivity and transcendence cultivated by culture's keepers has been designed to obscure its own antinomies, partisan positionings and the very sectarianism of the self/other divide.

The threat posed by the reassertion of the intersection of culture and politics, such as that argued in Naji al-Ali's cartoons, to a dominant ideology of authoritarian control is attested to by the violence and consistency of the policing reaction to such an intersection. Such policing has been marked, for example, by the implementation of censorship both overt and covert, from the McCarthy hearings in the United States in the 1950s to the rhetoric of "standards" and "basics" that had characterized the Reagan/Bush regimes' education policy and made it possible for one and the same man to qualify for the positions of both Secretary of Education and "drug czar." It has also included the Israeli military occupation's repeated closings of Palestinian universities and schools in the West Bank and Gaza Strip (particularly during the intifada), the official denial of a teaching post in 1974 to the historian Walter Rodney when he returned to his native Guyana, and the Salvadoran army's four-year occupation of the University of El Salvador from 1980 to 1984, as well as the assassination by right-wing death squads in November 1989 of six Jesuit priests in El Salvador's Central American University. The control of what Foucault referred to as the "circulation, manipulation and composition" of cultural production also extends to the imprisonment of dissident intellectuals and even, when necessary, to the assassination of the "authors."

The litany of committed intellectuals, partisans of organized resistance movements, who have been the victims of political assassination, bears witness to the coercive effectiveness of a dominant ideology of separatism and its need to eliminate those individuals in whose collaborative, secularizing work a space was elaborated for "the face of the future" – the conjunction of culture and political struggle – as well as to the creative potential of such a conjunction and the collective possibilities across self/other divides that that secularizing vision entails. The violent deaths of these intellectuals delineated and continues to demarcate in turn a critical site for a self-critique from within the resistance movements to which they contributed through their writing and work and a re-elaboration of strategies of resistance that has emerged out of the inquiry into the circumstances of their deaths: Naji al-Ali (Palestinian, died 1987); Malcolm X (African–American, died 1965); Amilcar Cabral (Guinea Bissau, died 1973); Steve Biko (South African, died 1977); Walter Rodney (Guyana, died 1980); Archbishop Oscar Romero

(Salvadoran, died 1980); Ignacio Ellacuría (died, 1989); Roque Dalton (Salvadoran, died 1975); Ghassan Kanafani (Palestinian, died 1972); and Ruth First (South African, died 1982).

> But alas! sacrifice is not a political argument and martyrdom does not constitute proof. When the list of martyrs grows long, when every act of courage is converted into martyrdom, it is because something is wrong. And it is just as much a moral duty to seek out the cause as it is to pay homage to the murdered or imprisoned comrades.
>
> Régis Debray (1968), *Revolution in the Revolution?*

The assassination of political writers, artists and intellectuals raises a number of significant questions with regard to the very nature of the investigation into their deaths. Beyond the most immediate question, "who killed . . .?", there is a further set of issues implied in the attempted responses to such a question, issues that challenge both the investigator and the research itself: what does it mean to ask, "who killed . . .?" – and what are the consequences that attend upon the asking of the question, "who killed . . .?"? What kind of examination is required in constructing an answer to these questions? The question posed in the terms of "who killed . . .?" entails for the investigator a kind of detective function, according to which a murderer-assassin must be identified, apprehended and "brought to justice." The traditional "whodunit" narrative paradigm provides a literary model based on the structural prerequisites of "law and order" for the narrative of such an investigation. The political or ideological function, by contrast, that asks not after the "who?" but into the "how and why?" that they were killed, not only redefines the "crime" but reconstructs the very elements of history and agency that are constitutive of it. Unlike the detective function, the systemic or ideological response to political assassination involves an interrogation of the state apparatuses that have determined the nature of crime itself, proposing thereby a narrative that challenges the past in its demands for a review of history and charts alternative possibilities for the future in its critical rethinking of the contradictions and conflicts of that past.

These two functions, the detective and the political or

ideological, are, for example, differently assigned and alternatively defined in *Murder in Mexico*, the report on the investigation into the assassination of Leon Trotsky in Mexico City on 20 August 1940, or what Isaac Deutscher (1963) has referred to as the "Hell-Black Night." At the time of Trotsky's death, the report's author, Leandro Sanchez Salazar, was Mexican Chief of Secret Police. In the introduction to his personal account of the police mission the official describes his role in the investigation as well as his own investment in the work:

> Destiny ordained that there should be a gap in my long career as a soldier to allow me to occupy the post of Mexican Chief of Police. I threw myself into this work with great enthusiasm. Police investigations thrilled me. I realized that I had the makings of a good detective, and, with the loyal collaboration of my assistants, soon got used to the work and devoted all my energy to it. And thus it fell to my lot to investigate the final tragedy of Don Leon, as, with respect and admiration, I called Trotsky. (Salazar, 1950, p. ix)

Julian Gorkin, by contrast, who assisted Sanchez Salazar in his narrative reconstruction of the police investigation, emphasizes rather the different significance for him of the ideological opposition to Stalinism at the time that such an inquiry enabled. Gorkin's introduction to *Murder in Mexico* which follows that of Sanchez Salazar, while not eschewing his own personal implication in the investigatory process, nonetheless foregrounds instead the alternative possibilities of the hegemonic and the counter-hegemonic political positionings and conflicts contained in the question, "who killed . . .?":

> I have never been attracted by police work, for I have too often been its victim, but in these circumstances my disinterested aid was a duty. I took a deep interest in the enquiry. It was, in fact, really engrossing, for it consisted of a battle against Stalinism and its methods. I was only continuing a struggle started at the time of my break with the Comintern in 1929, a struggle which had already cost me so much bitterness. As will be seen, it was not yet finished. (pp. xv–xvi)

The subversive consequences of this combined investigation and report by both police chief (albeit an exceptional one) and ideologue are further emphasized by the delay imposed on the publication of Sanchez Salazar's *Murder in Mexico* by the circumstances of the Second World War and Stalin's alliance at the time with the Western powers, a delay also related to the deferral of the release of Trotsky's own book on Stalinism until, as Gorkin reports, a more "opportune" moment (p. xviii). As Deutscher (1963) points out in his biography of Trotsky, already in 1936, many of Trotsky's sympathizers were inhibited in the expression of their support for him by the "simple-minded fear of aiding Hitler by criticizing Stalin" (p. 369). And while Trotsky planned for the establishment of a Fourth International, the Comintern itself was anticipating its own dissolution, which followed three years after Trotsky's fated demise.

The controversy, then, surrounding the investigation and its published report of Trotsky's assassination – as much even as the assassination itself – makes manifest the critical enterprise and its political ramifications, from the national to the international, that ultimately inhere in the question, "who killed . . .?" and its translations into an inquiry as to the "how and why?". The investigation itself becomes an intervention into the existing relationships of political power with consequences for the positioning of the principal investigators and their own political situations.

Assassination has been variously defined over the ages by political scientists, historians and legal advisors to monarchs, by rulers both legitimate and illegitimate, and governments and their agencies and agents provocateurs. The term itself, "assassination," is generally traced to an Ismaili Shi'ite sect that operated in Syria and Iran in the eleventh and twelfth centuries. Known as the *hashishiyun* (whence the designation "assassins"), the members of this group were reputed to slay their opponents with a bravado that was popularly attributed to their use of drugs. More recently, however, the legal and political definitions of assassination have been debated and refined in order to accommodate both the pressures of contemporary circumstances and, just as significantly, the demands of the system that seeks to

contain the challenges to its authority within its legal and political jurisdiction. The political scientists Havens, Leiden and
Schmitt, for example, in *The Politics of Assassination*, written in
1970 following a period of recurrent international assassinations, define assassination as the "deliberate, extralegal killing of
an individual for political purposes" (p. 4). The case studies that
they present in their account of assassination range without distinction or qualification from Verwoerd in South Africa and
Somoza in Nicaragua to Patrice Lumumba of the Congo and
Martin Luther King in the United States, a collocation presum-
ably designed to demonstrate an ostensibly objective neutrality
concerning the politics of assassination. That neutrality, however,
betrays its own partisan positioning in the authors' expression of
their abiding concern for the "systemic impacts produced by
assassination," their concern, that is, with assassination as an
untoward, "extralegal" disruption of the *status quo*.

Franklin Ford's subsequent study, *Political Murder* (1985),
assumes a similarly "neutral" position in its presentation of the
history of assassination, from the regicides of ancient Egypt and
Israel to contemporary acts of "terrorism." Ford, however,
locates his neutrality in that same historicizing of the phenome-
non of "political murder" and its centuries-long development,
revealing in the volume's subtitle the political program that
informs the ideological trajectory of his reconstructed historical
narrative: "from tyrannicide to terrorism." Ford defines assassination as the "intentional killing of a specified victim or group of
victims, perpetrated for reasons related to his (her, their) public
prominence and undertaken with a political purpose in view" (p.
2). In his adjudication of contemporary assassinations, however,
Ford marks a shift, the move "from tyrannicide to terrorism," in
what he has delineated in the history of assassination as "political purpose" and concludes that "what remains [today] is
behavior, stripped of political trappings. And of behavior that is
murderous, whatever its partisan claims, one must ask: What
about political life?" (p. 240) In thus cordoning off, on alleged
historical grounds, what counts as "political" and what does
not, the "political" itself becomes only that which can be accom-
modated within the parameters of the dominant ideology and its
legislation of that same construction of the "political." Ford's

analysis of the modern world thus exempts assassinations carried out by the state or its paramilitary branches from public political scrutiny. It also disallows investigation into the events of state-sponsored "terror" (such as the US's "School of Assassins" – or School of the Americas) and their legacy: a legacy of opposition and resistance, of organized protest against such abuses of power, that might serve to regenerate the very strategies that the state-committed assassination programs had sought to eradicate.

The much-heralded "death of the author," then, the assassi-nation of writers and authors, cannot always be reduced or for that matter sublimated to a metaphorical or even literary phe-nomenon. Rather, the assassination of the writer is a historical and political event with very tangible cultural, critical and mate-rial consequences for theorizing the subsequent participation in and reclamation of the work of intellectual figures who have been instrumental in organizing resistance to systems and dis-courses of domination, and whose life work had been committed to redefining the very "politics of shed blood."

In his essay, "National Liberation and Culture," delivered at Syracuse University in 1970 as the first Eduardo Mondlane Memorial Lecture, Amilcar Cabral addressed his audience with the appeal, "If we manage to persuade the African freedom fight-ers and all those concerned for freedom and progress of the African peoples of the conclusive importance of this question [of the relation between the national liberation struggle and culture] in the process of struggle, we shall have paid significant homage to Eduardo Mondlane." In concluding his address, Cabral returned to the assassination of the former president of Mozambique's resistance movement, Frelimo, murdered by agents of the Portuguese government in 1969:

> One might say that Eduardo Mondlane was *savagely* assassi-nated because he was capable of identifying with the culture of his people, with their deepest aspirations, through and against all attempts or temptations for the alienation of his personality as an African and a Mozambican. Because he had forged a new cul-ture in the struggle, he fell as a combatant. (p. 154, Cabral's emphasis)

In this contextualization of his remarks on culture and struggle within the history of Mondlane's assassination, Cabral insists on their political and ideological significance in understanding the reconstruction of the resistance movement and in recharting its agenda of liberation. While the essay "National Liberation and Culture" stands on its own as an important contribution to the complex debate (including, for example, Frantz Fanon's analysis of culture and political violence in *The Wretched of the Earth*) on the function of national culture in organizing resistance to colonial domination, the narrative frame of Mondlane's assassination is itself critical to the essay's intervention into the terms of that debate. Cabral grounds historically within that frame his already-historicized theoretical formulations of the role of culture, developed out of the specific material conditions of the resistance, in the national liberation struggle.

Just four years after he delivered his homage to Eduardo Mondlane, Cabral himself was assassinated in Conakry by members of his own Guinea Bissau resistance organization, the Partido Africano da Independencia de Guine e Cabo Verde (PAIGC), working in collaboration with the Portuguese military regime. While Cabral had always maintained that "we are all necessary to the struggle, but no one is indispensable" (cited in Chabal, 1983, p. 142), his death was critical to the subsequent history of the national liberation struggle in Portugal's African colonies. Liberation would come to Guinea Bissau a year later, in 1975, but the means to that liberation as well as to its developments in ensuing years were conditioned significantly by Cabral's leadership and his unanticipated death.

As Chabal wrote in his posthumous intellectual and political biography of the PAIGC leader, a study in which the fact of Cabral's untimely death once again provides the framework for a retrospective re-reading of the issues of "revolutionary leadership and people's war":

Revolutionary leaderships are sensitive to the deaths of party leaders both because leadership is usually a key to the success of their political action and because they often have no institutionalized mechanism to replace the leadership. In the early stages of a revolution, particularly, the loss of a strong leader may well change the unity and cohesion of the party itself. (p. 132)

Chabal goes on to examine the dynamics of the PAIGC on the eve of liberation and in the shadow of Cabral's death, as well as in the later developments of political independence and post-colonial cultural practices. Cabral's own philosophy of resistance in this context becomes crucial both to the enterprise of under-standing the motivation for his killing and to the party's structural and theoretical capacity to sustain its agenda of orga-nized political resistance after his death. Critical to Cabral's philosophy had been the international vision of emancipation that he represented from within Africa in the combined resistance movements of Cape Verde and Guinea Bissau as well as globally in his emphasis on the necessarily collective and combined strug-gle of Africans and the Portuguese working class against imperialist exploitation.

Basil Davidson, in his tribute to Cabral in 1984 on the occa-sion of the tenth anniversary of the African leader's death, reiterated that vision: "The true vocation of these new nations – true in the sense of the capacity to yield a further process of development – was to overcome the colonial heritage by moving 'beyond nationalism'." Why, Davidson goes on to ask, "should a revolutionary nationalism not grow in time, organically, regionally, into an internationalism?" (p. 43). Davidson's essay, "On Revolutionary Nationalism: The Legacy of Cabral," focuses on Cabral's contributions to what was then the First World's theorizing of resistance. In this it shifts the emphasis from Patrick Chabal's study which had centered on the African context for inquiring into the significance of the assassination of Amilcar Cabral. Davidson, however, reminds his audience that it is to Africa that the First World strategist must by turns look in order to sustain the political and cultural legacy that Cabral, in his struggle and in his death, had bequeathed.

Davidson's re-reading of that critically dynamic legacy opens with two components of Cabral's thinking: the concept of a colo-nial petty bourgeois leadership which must commit "class suicide" in its class consciousness (and class interests), and the argument that any real liberation must itself be a process of revolutionary struggle. These two directives taken from Cabral's strategy of resistance also contribute to an understanding of Cabral's own death at the hands of an assassin in that that death itself, its circumstances and its perpetrators, revealed the decided failure of the colonial petty bourgeoisie to rethink and revision its own historical role. Davidson proposes rather to relocate Cabral's death by assassination through a re-examination of its significance in a "process of revolution." Significantly, then, it was Cabral's own explicit acknowledgement of internationalism that Davidson sees as crucial to his legacy, and its critical reversal of a linear narrative that moved historically from center to periphery. Pointing to Cabral's engaged work with the Portuguese situation and the elements that historically constituted it, Davidson asks, "Whenever before had revolutionary change in Africa helped to promote revolutionary change in Europe? Hadn't 'all the books' declared that such a thing was impossible, even unthinkable? Yet it happened, and this was another part of the legacy of Cabral" (p. 23).

At the trial in South Africa in 1976 of Steve Biko, the leader of the Black Consciousness movement, on charges of "alleged subversion by intent," a singular aspect of the prosecutor's examination of the defendant focused on the death by assassination of Nthuli Shezi, who had been the vice-president of the Black People's Convention (BPC). The prosecutor brought as incriminating evidence against Biko the wording of the tribute to Shezi issued by the BPC: "The violent assassination was inflicted by an agent of protection of white racism, superiority and oppression on our black brother. It should not be regarded as being directed towards him alone, but should be regarded as an assault on the entire black community" (cited in Woods, 1987, p. 201). More incriminating still as evidence of Biko's subversive intentions was the defendant's own attendance at Shezi's funeral:

Attwell: Did you attend Shezi's funeral?
Biko: I was there, yes.
Attwell: Was it an emotional funeral?
Biko: All funerals are emotional.
Attwell: What sort of speeches were delivered?

Biko: There were speeches to encourage people to continue. It is the typical African situation, when anybody of note dies the normal theme of the speeches there is that what he was doing other people must continue with. That was the theme of the white minister who conducted the funeral.

Attwell: You say it was a white minister who conducted the funeral?

Biko: Yes, it was.

Attwell: I submit to you that the speakers brought out all the good in Mr Shezi, whatever good there may have been, and neglected any weak points that he may have had.

Biko: This is done.

Attwell: And brought out all the evil things they could about the whites, and ignored all the good there may or may not be. Would you agree with me?

Biko: I think they have not finished all the evil. (Woods, 1987, p. 202)

Steve Biko's own death in detention in 1977 importantly assisted in producing another kind of cross-examination, one designed to interrogate the South African apartheid system as a whole – as this system was consummately summed up in its prison apparatus. The official inquest into the physical causes and personal responsibility for Biko's death while in detention did not culminate at any time in any indictment, much less punishment, of guilty parties in his assassination, because, as Donald Woods puts it, "the State had not seen fit to indict anyone for the death of Steve Biko, it becomes necessary to indict the State" (p. 355). Following the inquest, however, and in response partly to international protest, the South African government did finally appoint a commission of inquiry headed by Justice Rabie to investigate the conditions of detention, and in particular political detention, in South Africa. The conclusions of the Rabie Report did expose some of the individual collapses, infringements and miscarriages of justice; nonetheless, it upheld the overall authority of the legal system and its penal apparatus. The report, further distinguished for the egregious selectivity of its sources of information and testimony, carefully avoiding the testimony or evidence of even a single former detainee, made a number of important recommendations that were eventually translated into law, including the Internal Security Act 1982 allowing for four types of detention without trial.

In the meantime, South African deaths in detention multiplied, including that of the trade unionist Neil Aggett in 1982, following which the Detainees' Parents Support Committee was established. Five years later, in 1987, three independent researchers from the University of Cape Town, Don Foster, Dennis Davis and Diane Sandler, published their own report on torture in South African prisons. Designed to be a response to the Rabie Commission's official government-sponsored inquiry, *Detention and Torture in South Africa* is itself a kind of commemoration of Steve Biko's assassination in detention and the indictment of the state that Biko's comrades had called for. In the testimony of several former detainees cited in the report, the example of Steve Biko figures prominently, critically displaying the attempt on the part of the state interrogators to appropriate once again from the popular narrative their own ultimate control and authority over the investigation – and its story – into the circumstances of the South African leader's violent death. According to one former prisoner:

> I was asked where I was going, and I told them that I was going to Sterkspruit for a holiday, and then I was taken to another office where there was a picture of Steve Biko. Then I was asked if I know this guy, and I say yes, that I know him. And they asked me where he is now, and I told them that he is dead. And they said that I will follow him if I don't speak the truth. (p. 130)

Another prisoner told again a similar story of his experience of questioning:

> Because it was just after that Biko thing and they also told me, You know how Biko died? So we are going to take it seriously. After – they say people are trying to escape. (p. 147)

In recontextualizing these excerpts of the prison system's interrogation of political prisoners within an investigation into the prison system itself, *Detention and Torture in South Africa* offers an alternative future, another legacy – if a posthumous one – to Biko's work and his death. That death then becomes a part of the investigation into conditions of political detention throughout the world. As Mario Hector would write from *Death Row* in Jamaica in 1984, "A new vibe emanated from this genesis of resistance" (p. 36).

In 1968, the Guyanese historian and theorist of Europe's under-development of Africa, Walter Rodney, was barred from re-entering Jamaica where he had been teaching at the University of the West Indies following his two-year assignment in Tanzania. Twelve years later, Rodney was assassinated in his native Guyana where, as in Jamaica, he had been prevented from assuming the teaching post he had returned from Africa to undertake. The actual circumstances of Rodney's death are well known, but the reasons for it, the calculations behind it and the consequences that ensued still remain controversial and con-flicted. According to Pierre Michel Fontaine, citing a sworn statement by Donald Rodney, Walter Rodney's brother, "a gov-ernment plant, Gregory Smith, an electronic expert and covert member of the Guyana Defense Force, had given Walter a two-way radio and advised him to go and test it in a particular area near the Georgetown prison. Apparently the bomb that the mur-derer(s) had placed inside the device being tested was triggered by a radio signal" (Fontaine, 1982, p. 42). The Guyanese govern-ment claimed for its own disinguous part that the technological ignorance and lack of sophistication on the part of the writer and revolutionary historian himself had brought about his untimely death.

If the government's account of the assassination is still hardly credible, the death of Walter Rodney, the author of *How Europe Underdeveloped Africa* (1974), occasioned important critical reassessments among his comrades and colleagues of Rodney's own historical significance and the history of counter-hegemonic resistance more generally. In investigating Rodney's death and its attendant injunctions for charting alternative trajectories, the historian's own admonitions, cited by Douglas Ferguson, are perhaps incumbent on his successors: "Make certain the history you produce is the result of the application of the analytical tools and not the imposition of conclusions from elsewhere" (Ferguson, 1982, p. 101). If Patrick Chabal had seen in Amilcar Cabral's assassination the fortuitous conjuncture of happenstance with the leader's "personality and his style of leadership [and] the structure of the PAIGC as a whole" (Chabal, 1983, p. 135), C. L. R. James elicited a similar problematic from the conditions of Rodney's death. James (1982) asked not only "who?": "The assassin, I believe, has disappeared. He was an agent of the Burnham government. Everyone has talked about the murder, but they have not talked about *that*" (p. 140), but James also wanted to know "why?" With this other question, James raised a further debate about Walter Rodney's assassination, one that summoned a larger political analysis of the structures of leadership and the collective responsibilities of the organization itself: "Rodney," James claimed, "should never have been there. No political leader had any right to be there. Not only should he never have been there, the people around him should have seen to it that he was not in any such position. That was a fundamental mistake, and it was a political mistake" (1982, p.139).

Rodney, though, had looked to James's response to his death when he recalled the influence of James on his own "life and thought." Speaking with colleagues in the United States in 1974–5 shortly before his return to Guyana, Rodney recollected that:

later on, at the university in Jamaica, C. L. R. James did exercise this force as a kind of model figure. And more recently, in my own life and thought, he's remained a model in a specific kind of way, not in the sense that I feel any commitment to pursue positions which he has adopted *per se*. But, as he has grown older – and as I have looked around me and recognized how the struggle creates so many casualties (and somehow along the line physiology plays a part) and how the older people get the more they seem to opt out of any revolutionary struggle, seem to wane, seem to take up curious positions that are actually reversals of where they earlier stood – James has become a model of the possibilities of retaining one's intellectual and ideological integrity over a protracted period of time. In other words, I've always said to myself that I hoped that at his age, if I'm around, I still

have some credibility as a progressive, that people wouldn't look
around and say, "This used to be a revolutionary". (p. 16)

That credibility could be neither special nor specious, however,
and for Rodney it was to be garnered across several fields –
including the academic. Recalling his work in the British university system, Rodney would maintain critically, even self-critically,
that:

> [t]here is a certain distance which one has to go in trying to meet
> the so-called standards. But beyond that it becomes self-defeating
> and ridiculous. And the question is, where is the cut-off point? To
> claim that the standards are irrelevant is never really to attack the
> world of bourgeois scholarship. Rather, it is simply to leave it in
> the hands of the enemy, as it were. (p. 25)

The task, then, that followed for other researchers on the occasion of Walter Rodney's assassination is more than academic.
According to Ewart Thomas, those inquirers into the manifold
question of "Who killed Walter Rodney?" are enjoined now to
"go into our various disciplines and attack the myths and distortions that result from the dominance of Eurocentric
scholarship in these disciplines" (p. 40). This task involves, as C.
L. R. James had maintained at the time, the research of politics
as much as it does the politics of research: "I hope somebody will
make it his business to write a thesis on what happened in the
Guyana revolution and the death of Walter Rodney, which is not
just the death of a singular and remarkable individual. It is a
whole political problem that is involved there, and I would like
you to look at it that way" (Alpers and Fontaine, 1982, p. 144).
    Guyana's independence came in 1966, following a protracted
contest among representations of race, economics and ideology,
and working both with local political exigencies and under the
international auspices of the United Nations' professed commitment to decolonization and its documentation of the rights of
colonized peoples. Twenty and more years later, though, as
anthropologist Brackette Williams (1991) would write, there
were still "stains on [the] name, war in [the] veins," and the
politics of socialist promises, ethnic divisiveness, territorial

nationalism and cultural heterogeneity continued to disrupt the Guyanese claims to self-determination and independence.

"A whole political problem," in James's words, it remains meanwhile, for it has not always been that writers have been singled out for death, nor that they have died alone. And the question of accountability, answerability, often strains the account of their demises. The death of Bobby Sands, an Irish republican prisoner on hunger strike in Long Kesh, on 5 May 1981, was followed by the deaths of nine fellow prisoners on strike with him: Francis Hughes (12 May), Raymond McCreesh (21 May), Patsy O'Hara (21 May), Joe McDonnell (8 July), Martin Hurson (13 July), Kevin Lynch (1 August), Kieran Doherty (2 August), Tom McIlwee (8 August), and Mickey Devine (20 August). Was this assassination? And who was responsible? The IRA hunger strike raises critical questions about agency, responsibility, answerability and accountability. Much as C. L. R. James had asked "why?" Walter Rodney died, the Irish hunger strikers posed the very questions of their own role in their protracted dying. Was their slow starvation assassination? or suicide, as Margaret Thatcher and the Church claimed? The republican prisoners were striking for the restoration of their political status. Although that status had not been officially restored by the British authorities when the strike was ended in October 1981, Bobby Sands had meanwhile served briefly as an elected member of Parliament, and Sinn Fein had crucially and decisively re-entered the realm of political participation in conjunction with its continued commitment to armed struggle for the liberation of Ireland. *Nor Meekly Serve My Time* (1994), the collected recollections of surviving prisoners from that period a decade ago, edited by Brian Campbell, Laurence McKeown and Felim O'Hagan, narrates the five years of protest demanding political recognition that led up to the 1981 hunger strikes, from the blanket protest through the no wash protest – and ultimately the deaths of ten men. Its contributors are from the ranks of the "Blanketmen" themselves, prisoners who now emerge as "historians, people who not only changed history but were themselves changed by it" (p. xvi). No less than Amilcar Cabral, Steve Biko or Walter Rodney, the "ten men dead" on hunger strike in a

British prison in the north of Ireland were, it has been argued, assassinated by the same official determinations that refused to recognize their political demands, and insisted that their political status should not be acknowledged. "Nor meekly serve my time," the title of the prisoners' memoirs of that collective assassination, is taken from the chorus of the song written in 1976, when "status" was rescinded, by Francie Brolly:

So I'll wear no convict's uniform
Nor meekly serve my time
That Britain might brand Ireland's fight
Eight hundred years of crime.

And yet, as Bernadette Devlin McAliskey – who had outlived the attempt on her life in 1983 – would write in the foreword to the testimonies of the hunger strikers' comrades, "'Greater love than this no man hath than he lay down his life for his friend.' Maybe I'm not sure how to deal with that degree of love. Maybe I wonder why they died for us, and we didn't die for them" (p. xiv).

The question of "why they died" would be repeated once again, eight years later, in El Salvador, following the mass murders at the UCA. According to the terse account provided by Lieutenant José Ricardo Espinoza, the order had been to eliminate the "intellectual leaders" of the guerrillas (cited in Whitfield, 1995, p. 9). Espinoza, once a student of the Jesuits and now a member of the infamous Atlacatl Battalion of the Salvadoran army, had participated in the murders of six Jesuit priests and their housekeeper and her daughter. The assassinations on the night of 16 November 1989, five days after the beginning of the major FMLN offensive of that year, was carried out on the grounds of their residence at the University of Central America (UCA). Fathers Ignacio Ellacuría, the university's rector, and Ignacio Martín-Baró, its vice-rector, Segundo Montes, Amando López, Juan Ramón Moreno, Joaquín López y López were murdered, along with Elba and Celina Ramos. Intellectuals the priests unequivocally were, and the Ramoses, mother and daughter, who died with them, were for their part representatives of the priests' own mission in El Salvador. Other massacres, to be sure, at the hands of the Salvadoran army during the last decade of civil war had preceded theirs: tens of thousands of Salvadorans across the city and throughout the countryside; and other priests as well – Father Rutilio Grande in the village of Aguilares in March 1977, Archbishop Oscar Romero as he delivered his homily at mass on 25 March 1980, and four North American religious women in December of that same year. Vilified by the Salvadoran army and its government and their no less complicitous supporters (including representatives of several US administrations), as "Marxist," "subversive," "theologians of liberation," the popular church in El Salvador had indeed espoused a historical mission, effectively, defiantly – and very differently – articulated by both Romero and Ellacuría, that committed them to a combined "option of the poor" and the Salvadoran "national reality."

For Romero, that commitment had come late, following the murder of Rutilio Grande, an assassination since referred to by many as the "miracle of Rutilio," in forming Romero's vision of his country's needs and the appeals of its people. The very titles of the four pastoral letters written by Romero during his three short years as Archbishop of San Salvador, however, indicate the renewed direction and political development that his last work had assumed as the "voice of the voiceless:" "The Easter Church" (April 1977); "The Church, The Body of Christ in History" (August 1977); "The Church and Popular Political Organizations" (August 1978); and finally "The Church's Mission amid the National Crisis" (August 1979). Only a month before he died, on 17 February 1980, Romero had written to the then US President Jimmy Carter, asking for his help – by limiting aid to El Salvador's military government – in protecting the human rights of El Salvador's people. And in his homily in the metropolitan cathedral on the Sunday before his death, the Archbishop had openly demanded of the Salvadoran military: *Cese la represión!* Those last words, "stop the repression," on 24 March 1980, were interrupted by the gunshot that killed him (see Romero, 1985).

Even as Romero's homily had been cut short by his assassination, so also Ignacio Ellacuría's mediating work on behalf of dialogue and negotiations between the Salvadoran government and the FMLN, was halted by his assassins. Already in 1969, in remarks entitled "Ponencia sobre vida religiosa y tercer mundo" and delivered in Madrid, Ellacuría had argued that the "third world is the prophetic denunciation of how badly arranged are the things of this world" (cited in Whitfield, 1995, p. 41). Those political negotiations which Ellacuría endorsed and for which he struggled and died would eventually lead three years later to the the Peace Accords signed in Chapultepec, Mexico, on 16 January 1992. Paradoxically, then, as Alvaro de Soto, the United Nations negotiator throughout the Salvadoran peace talks, would argue, "the story of the negotiation, yet to be written, will have to interlock with the Jesuit murder story from which it cannot be separated" (foreword to Whitfield, 1995, p. xii). The end of the Jesuits' lives, it could be claimed, was yet another beginning. According to Romero, in a June 1979 homily, "It would be sad if in a country where they are killing so terribly, we did not count priests among the victims" (cited in Whitfield, 1995, p. 99). But the slain Jesuits' colleague at the UCA, Jon Sobrino, who was in Thailand at the time of their deaths, would shortly afterwards recall the critical moment of receiving the news of the slaughter:

> At the other end of the telephone, in London, was a great friend of mine and of all the Jesuits in El Salvador, a man who has shown great solidarity with our country and our church. He began with these words: "Something terrible has happened." "I know," I replied, "Ellacuría." But I did not know. He asked me if I was sitting down and had something to write with. I said I had and then he told me what had happened. "They have murdered Ignacio Ellacuría." I remained silent and did not write anything, because I had already been afraid of this. But my friend went on: "They have murdered Segundo Montes, Ignacio Martín-Baró, Amando López, Juan Ramón Moreno, and Joaquin López y López." My friend read the names slowly and each of them reverberated like a hammer blow that I received in total helplessness. I was writing them down, hoping that the list would end after each name. But after each name came another, on to the end. The whole community, my whole community had been murdered. In addition, two women had been murdered with them. (Sobrino and Ellacuría, 1990, p. 5)

"Something to write with": making once again – before as after the fact – the all-too-pained connection between writing and assassination.

More important perhaps than the question "who killed?" is the issue of how? and why? And when is the "opportune moment" for the examination of these questions? Roque Dalton was a Salvadoran poet, writer and partisan in the Ejercito Revolucionario del Pueblo (ERP) within the Salvadoran resistance movement. In 1975 Dalton, who opposed the militaristic agenda of some of ERPs members in favor of a prolonged people's war and more popular organizing on the ground prior to a major military operation, was ordered executed, in a decision whose consequences are still being played out, by those cadres with whom he had disagreed.

Three years earlier, in Beirut in July 1972, Ghassan Kanafani, a Palestinian writer, critic, novelist and journalist for the PFLP, was assassinated in a car-bomb explosion that also took the life of his twelve-year-old niece, Lamees. Mossad, the Israeli secret service, eventually claimed responsibility for the death of the "commando who never fired a gun," as one obituary described the Palestinian intellectual. Mossad's claim, however, relieved the Palestinian resistance of the kind of self-scrutiny that had followed on Naji al-Ali's assassination, or Roque Dalton's execution. Kanafani's radical political theorizing on behalf of a "democratic revolution" as the prerequisite for a "democratic secular state," an argument that had characterized his writing from the early novel *Men in the Sun* to his last essay on "the case of Abu Hamidu," raises again – and again – the question, If Ghassan Kanafani were alive today, would he be allowed to live? Nine months after his death, for example, Israeli commandos broke into the Beirut apartment of Kamal Nassar and shot him dead. Like Amilcar Cabral's internationalism, Steve Biko's black consciousness, Walter Rodney's class analysis of the world capitalist system and Roque Dalton's revisioning of militarism, Kanafani's critique of sectarianism was as anathema to recalcitrant forces in his own movement as it was to the Zionism of the state of Israel. The resistance movements themselves, and in turn the political and intellectual inheritors of these legacies, have

only begun the task of elaborating answers to the questions
posed by the "deaths of their authors," the assassinations of
their leadership.

Black Gold is a study of Mozambican migrant workers in the
mines of South Africa, published in 1983 under the name of
Ruth First, a white South African woman active in the ANC and
the South African Communist Party in the 1960s and 1970s. A
journalist and a historian of Africa as well, Ruth First had been
arrested during the Rivonia raids on the ANC in 1963 in South
Africa and sentenced under the 90 Day Detention Law. Her
prison memoir, *117 Days*, takes its title from this law which
allowed for automatic renewal of the detention period at the
discretion of the authorities. Eventually, following various banning orders and restrictions on her work, and later a period in
England where she co-authored a biography of Olive Schreiner
with Ann Scott, First went into her final exile in Mozambique.
Her activities as a researcher at Eduardo Mondlane University in
Maputo came to an end when she was assassinated by a parcel
bomb in August 1982. At Mondlane University, First had been
part of a large research collective studying migrant labor patterns
in the countries of Southern Africa and their effects on historical
transformations in the region's indigenous social structures. The
volume, entitled *Black Gold*, was part of that collaborative
research effort. It combines historical background and sociolog-
ical analysis of the "proletarianization of the peasantry,"
interviews with miners and their families, and work songs composed and sung by male migrants as well as by those men,
women and children who remained behind.

Black Gold was published posthumously in the year following
Ruth First's death, posthumously only if one considers the function of "author" according to the most limited definition of the
word, as referring to the personal identity of the authorial individual. The contribution of *Black Gold*, however, to a
reconstruction of political strategy and the ideology of literary
critical practice is manifold and includes an implicit critique of
authorship and the "task of the intellectual" in the resistance
struggle. The reformulation of genre, together with its textual
analyses of class and race in the migrant labor movement, which

confutes too sectarian a definition of "nationalism" as an enabling paradigm, are reiterated on a sociopolitical level over the issue of authorial identity – and another "politics of shed blood." The very circumstances of "exile" that had conditioned First's participation in the research project require a particular construction of nationalism and departures from it. Unlike her compatriot Nadine Gordimer, for example, for whom exile from South Africa has at times been novelistically construed either as escape to Europe, as in her novel *Burger's Daughter*, or as existential flight in the case of Maureen Smales's headlong plunge at the end of *July's People*, Ruth First would seem to have reworked the exile imposed by the South African state as continued participation in the popular history of African resistance. Ruth First's biographical narrative intersects with the labor history of the migrant worker and *Black Gold* can be read critically as an active, indeed committed, conflation of the two narrative modes, two historical paradigms, otherwise separated by disciplinary strictures and a cult of individual authorship. If *Black Gold* is read as the autobiography of the partisan intellectual subject in which a personal itinerary is assimilated into a larger historical narrative of resistance and struggle, then First's own exile – and death – become crucial as part of the means to the narration of the history of the migrant workers. Her political task as an intellectual is subsumed by the cooperative research project in which the laborers themselves acquire authorial voices and historical agency.

The issues of authorial identity and the work of the intellectual are defiantly reconstituted across national borders. Ruth First's identification, like that of Roque Dalton and Ghassan Kanafani, with the "faces of the present" provide the critical parameters for an analysis of the "face of the future." It also allows for a re-identification of the resistance movement within an expanded emancipatory agenda. Rather than their elevation uniquely as "writers, martyrs, revolutionaries," their work addresses the exigencies of criticism and the recreation of intellectual priorities. Their writings suggest too the multiple answers to the questions, "who killed?" and "how?" and "why?" and "when?" – answers to be located perhaps in a revisioning of the calculated antagonism of the dominant self/other paradigm into a collective and secularized struggle against sectarian exploitations.

A teeshirt popular in the occupied West Bank from the beginning of the Palestinian intifada carried on its back Naji al-Ali's "child of the camps," Hanzalla. On the front of the teeshirt was stencilled another Naji al-Ali cartoon in which a Hanzalla figure with *nahnu*, or "we," written on his back is shown reaping a field of wheat, whose shafts are drawn in the shape of *ana*, the Arabic word for "I." All of these biographies/obituaries were written in blood prior to 1990–91: before, that is, the fall of the Berlin Wall, the Gulf War, the dissolution of the Soviet Union, each of which crises configures part of a conjunctural closure to one era of "national liberation." And then there came Somalia, Rwanda, the former Yugoslavia. Other lists. That erstwhile "closure" enjoins at the same time a new urgency, a rewriting – and even if not in blood, a reprise at least of the radical secularist issues, of the emancipatory and visionary linkage of "civil rights" and a new "human rights," of "internationalism" – that these writers, martyrs, revolutionaries lived – and died – for. Naji al-Ali, Malcolm X, Amilcar Cabral, Steve Biko, Walter Rodney, Bobby Sands, Archbishop Romero, Ignacio Ellacuría – and Roque Dalton, Ghassan Kanafani, Ruth First: if they were alive today, would their erstwhile enemies not have found new collaborators, who in turn would find it just as necessary to assassinate them? And what would they have to say?

PART II

WRITERS, MARTYRS, REVOLUTIONARIES

History and Endings: Ghassan Kanafani and the Politics of Terminations in Palestine

Why didn't they bang on the walls of the truck?

When we set out from Jaffa for Acre there was nothing tragic about our departure. We were just like anybody who goes to spend the festival season every year in another city. Our time in Acre passed as usual, with nothing untoward. I was young then, and so I probably enjoyed those days because they kept me from going to school. But whatever the fact of the matter, the picture gradually became clearer on the night of the great attack on Acre. That night passed, cruel and bitter amidst the despondency of the men and the prayers of the women. You and I and others of our age were too young to understand what the story meant from beginning to end, but that night the threads began to grow clearer.
Ghassan Kanafani, "The Land of Sad Oranges" (1958) in *Men in the Sun and Other Palestinian Stories*

"To understand what the story meant from beginning to end" is the task that the Palestinian child had assigned to himself in "The Land of Sad Oranges," an early story by Ghassan Kanafani, in order to discover the answer to his dire question of "why we had become refugees." The Palestinian writer is himself engaged in the historical project of writing large that same intimate story. The complementary and coordinating narratives thus produced contribute to the historical record and enter into the very events and significant moments of the life of the Palestinian people: flight (*hurub*), exile (*ghurbah*), resistance (*muqawamah*), steadfastness (*sumud*), and ultimately the awaited, anticipated, but interminably deferred, return (*awdah*) to Palestine. The terms and the terminus do not coincide. The writer, however, not only describes the historical events and circumstances, but also provides a historical sense and identity for those who have lived through them. The writer, like the historian, according to Marc Ferro, (1975, p. 26) the French historiographer and cinematician, "has as his first task that of restoring to society the History of which the institutional apparatus deprived it. The primary duty, then, is to interrogate society, to listen to it. It is not enough to make use of the archives, one must above all create them, contribute to their constitution: film, question those who have never had the right to speak, never had the right to bear witness".

Since Arthur James Balfour wrote to Lord Rothschild on 2 November 1917 that "His Majesty's government view with favour the establishment in Palestine of a national home for the Jewish people, and will use their best endeavours to facilitate the achievement of this object" (Balfour Declaration), the Palestinian historical narrative has been at odds with another, imperially imposed, chronology and territorial design. Particular dates denote that dislocated story: the Palestinian uprising of 1936–39, the creation of the State of Israel in 1948, the Suez war of 1956, the June 1967 War, the October 1973 War, the Camp David Accords in 1978–9, the Israeli invasion of Lebanon in 1982, and the Palestinian intifada that began in December 1987. Was the now famous (or infamous) handshake between Yitzhak Rabin and Yasser Arafat in September 1993 that signed off on the "Declaration of Principles" between the two peoples to be as perfidious a terminus to that narrative as the extravagantly generous missive from Balfour to Rothschild had been earlier in the century? It is in particular the decisive period between 1956 and 1973 to which Ghassan Kanafani would contribute alternative formulations of struggle and historicity.

Whereas "The Land of Sad Oranges" describes a child's reaction to the first Palestinian exodus in 1948 at the time of the establishment of the Israeli state, Kanafani's short novel *Men in the Sun*, which appeared five years later in 1963, takes as its central issue a further phase of that exodus and consequent exile, the Palestinians' search for employment and a livelihood outside their homeland and in the traditionally conservative but oil-rich Arab states of the Gulf. *Men in the Sun*, according to Fadl al-Naqib's summary of the main plot development:

> is the story of three Palestinians who do not know each other but who find themselves in Basra [Iraq] at the same time where they each are trying illegally to cross the border into Kuwait. In Kuwait they hope to find work and a subsistence which they had had no hope of in the different lands from which they come. In Basra each of them discovers that he is unable to pay the price demanded by the professional smugglers, and each tries in his own way to find a means of exit, until finally all of them encounter each other and the self-appointed smuggler who offers to take them to Kuwait for a cut-rate price. This smuggler, called Abul Khaizuran, is the highly skilled driver of a large water truck belonging to a wealthy Kuwaiti merchant. The truck is not subjected to a search at the border.

Abul Khaizuran's plan for smuggling them out of Iraq and into Kuwait is a simple one. Since he is obliged in any case to return the now empty water truck to Kuwait, he can also take the three men with him. For most of the trip they can ride with him until just before the border when he will hide them inside the empty water tank. Once he has cleared his papers and driven a short distance past the border, they can get out and finish the trip next to him. The three Palestinians are not happy with this plan. Abu Qais, the oldest of them, has been unenthusiastic about the plan from the beginning, thinking that it is a hopeless and risky adventure. He is more inclined to go with the professional smugglers, even given the high price. Marwan, the youngest, has mixed feelings and is unable to make up his mind. Thus it falls to Assad, the most knowledgeable and experienced, to make the decision.

Assad, through his cleverness and knowledge, is able to get Abul Khaizuran to admit that his job is not really transporting water, but smuggling goods for the Kuwaiti merchant. Smuggling people is a side job of his own and it gives him company on the

long and tedious trip. Abul Khaizuran's admission doesn't influence Assad's decision, but it does give him the authority to get
Abu Qais and Marwan to agree to the decision he himself has
made. He accepts the risk because in fact he has no other choice.

Abul Khaizuran is in fact a smuggler, not an impostor, and he
believes that his plan can work, and furthermore that he is doing
a service to the others. He has done this before, successfully. On
this trip, however, Abul Khaizuran's luck turns bad. The bureaucrats at the border begin making obscene jokes to while away the
time in the desert sun. His efforts to escape the prattle of the
employers are futile and by the time he returns to his truck, drives
it some distance and stops to open the tank, it is too late. The
three men are dead, suffocated.

This is not the first time that Abul Khaizuran has had bad
luck. He is, after all, a Palestinian. In 1948, he was wounded in
one of the battles and as a result "lost his manhood." From then
on he has repeated to himself: "Manhood lost. Country lost.
And everything else in this cursed existence . . ." Abul Khaizuran
drives his truck to one of Kuwait's garbage dumps where he dis-
poses of the three bodies, but only after removing their
wristwatches. Before going back to his truck, he argues with a
thought in his mind. Finally, when he can resist it no longer, he
begins shouting: "Why didn't they bang on the walls of the truck?
Why?" (pp. 37–41)

Written in January 1962, in the course of a month in which
Kanafani remained hidden at home in Beirut because he had no
official papers or legal documentation (see Anni Kanafani,
1973), *Men in the Sun* is a topical work with a setting immediately relevant to the time and place of its composition and the
circumstances of its author. On one level, though, the novel can
be read as a political allegory, allegory in the strictest, even most
conventional literary critical, sense: a narrative, according to the
glossaries, "in which agents and actions, and sometimes the setting as well are contrived both to make coherent sense on the
'literal,' or primary, level of signification, and also to signify a
second, correlated order of agents, concepts and events"
(Abrams, 1981). According to such an allegorical reading, Abul
Khaizuran, the truck driver, represents the Palestinian leadership

at the time, emasculated and impotent, having "lost his man-hood" in 1948 in the first Arab–Israeli war surrounding the creation of the State of Israel. Although not without certain good intentions, his personal despair and moral weakness have cor-rupted him. He bargains over rates with the three Palestinians he has offered to transport to Kuwait and, once they are dead, avails himself of their wristwatches, removing them from the corpses he has disposed of by depositing them in the Kuwaiti garbage dump. Hajj Rida, who owns the truck driven by Abul Khaizuran, like the professional smugglers in Basra who over-charge their clients and refuse to guarantee their journey, exemplifies the Arab leaders and regimes who, all the while that they might have pretended to support the Palestinians in their struggle to secure their national future and to liberate their land, in fact exploit them for their own opportunistic ends. Indeed, the Palestinians had often referred to themselves as "Uthman's shirt," in reference to the bloodied shirt of the martyred Arab caliph in the early days of Islam which was carried as a banner into battle in order to arouse the enthusiasm and maintain the zeal of the troops (see Johnson, 1982). Meanwhile, centuries later, the Arab leaders continue to pursue their pleasures, vicari-ous and otherwise, whether in hunting, like Hajj Rida, or through the obscene stories which titillate the petty functionaries who sit idly behind desks, frustrating the lives of other people who must court their favor and await their favors. Finally, in the scheme of the allegory, Abu Qais, Assad and Marwan, the "men in the sun," are the Palestinian people, ignorant, naïve, living in a past which no longer exists and dreaming of a future which they have neither the knowledge nor the power to bring into being – much less the wherewithal even to bang on the walls of the truck's tank.

The possibilities for, and the coherence of, an allegorical inter-pretation of the novel notwithstanding, and for all its political motivation, *Men in the Sun* is not simply a tract, nor is it just a manifesto or a piece of reductive propaganda. Nor would one, as Frank O'Connor (1963, p. 58) had formulated the limitations of political allegory, "like to think that something that moves only from within is really being moved from outside by the desire to teach a lesson". Fadl al-Naqib, Kanafani's friend and critic, once took issue with what he saw as the writer's undue preoccupation with the pressing exigencies of the present: "He spent his time on innumerable issues, but he wrote in an everyday fashion. For us [young aspiring writers], the whole question of publication was a special one, for a distant future, wrapped in dreams. For him, however, what he wrote today he wrote to be published tomorrow"(1983, p. 14). Ghassan Kanafani, a journalist as well as a novelist, "lived," according to Fadl al-Naqib, "without dreaming." His works, however, are not without a vision, and his critique of the contemporary Palestinian reality was directed at the futile passivity of many of its dreams. Abu Qais, Assad and Marwan, as revealed in the flashbacks intercalated throughout the short novel, are seeking a legendary Promised Land, a place where their dreams will at long last be realized and where they will be liberated once and for all from the yoke of oppression and exploitation which had too long characterized their lives. In Kuwait, Abu Qais hopes to find the money to send his children to school, to buy a small house and perhaps even one or two olive shoots. Marwan, who has had to leave school, is looking for learning and experience. Finally, for Assad, Kuwait means freedom: freedom from his uncle who wants him to marry his daughter. These socially contained perspectives, then, are the dreams they dream, each one "swallowed up in his own thoughts. The huge lorry was carrying them along the road, together with their dreams, their failures, their hopes and ambitions, their misery and despair, their strength and weakness, their past and future, as if it were pushing against the immense door to a new, unknown destiny, and all eyes were fixed on the door's surface as though bound to it by invisible threads" (p. 46).

The resigned passivity associated with an acquiescing acceptance of fate's ultimatums and decrees is the fatal curse of the "men in the sun." When the novel opens, Abu Qais is bending his ear to the ground listening to the echoes of his own heartbeat resonating from the damp earth. In front of him is the Shatt al-Arab. And "on the other side of this Shatt, just the other side, were all the things he had been deprived of. Over there was Kuwait. What only lived in his mind existed there" (p. 13). Kneeling to the ground, before the gates of the Promised Land, Abu Qais recalls his son's schoolteacher in their village who, unlike all the previous schoolteachers, could not lead the villagers in their prayers, much to their surprise. "What do you do then?" they asked him. "Many things," the schoolteacher answered, "I'm a good shot for instance" (p. 11). The traditional leadership of Palestine, the imams, the shaykhs and the muftis, like the heads of the family and the nobles of the clan, must, it is suggested, give way to a new organization, on this side of dreams, if their revolution is to come true.

Each of the "men in the sun," meanwhile, has arrived at the Iraq–Kuwait border leaving behind not only the dispossession of refugee life but also a broken or disrupted family tradition. Abu Qais's son, for example, has been educated by Ustaz Selim, the schoolteacher trained in the use of weapons. The boy's knowledge of the world contradicts his father's ignorance and challenges the tenets of patriarchal authority. Assad, on the other hand, is fleeing the cultural traditions of conservative Palestinian society which insists on arranging the marriages for its children. Marwan, in turn, must find in Kuwait the means to provide for his mother who has been deserted not only by her husband for another woman, but by her eldest son who, already working in the Gulf, has ceased sending the remittances necessary to support the family he left behind. Immanent in Kanafani's novel is the transition from what, in Edward Said's terminology (1981, pp. 12ff.), might be called traditional, orthodox associations based on the pieties of "filiation" to an organization having its foundations in the political bonds and analytical allegiances of "affiliation" – in other words, a nascent Palestinian resistance movement. It is neither Kuwait, the Promised Land, nor a return to the traditional ways of the past, which will answer to the demands of these men for a self-determined place in history. The rhetoric of appeasement and resignation, like the walls of the water tank, must be disassembled, made to speak another language, in a vocabulary that will pierce those confines. Words, terminations, according to the Palestinian writer, Fawaz Turki, thus become:

> interlaced with the perception of current history and the vehemence of existence. The Gulf. Employment in the Gulf. Everybody's brother, everybody's father is in the Gulf working for

oil companies. Fathers and brothers go away for years on end to the only place in the Arab world that allows Palestinians to work. Your brother works his guts out in the *desert* to send you to school, a mother says. *Desert* becomes more than a word, and acquires the added mystical significance of fathers and elder brothers separated from their families, of a whole world of ennui, intense heat, aloneness that children knew awaited them when they grew up to earn a living. *Desert*, like *gendarmes*, like the *Aliens Department*, like *work permits*, were entities that had an element of terror to them that was your lot because you had nowhere else to go. (1988, p. 11, emphasis in original)

Is this semantic training, then, what it would take, as the child from the "land of sad oranges" was eventually to learn, "to understand what the story meant from beginning to end"?

When Tawfiq Salih, the Egyptian film director, made a feature film of *Men in the Sun* eight years after the literary work's publication, he altered the story's ending even while remaining faithful to the rest of the novel's action, not least to its narrative complications and flashbacks. While Abul Khaizuran is held a captive of the bureaucrats' sordid wit, the director moves his camera from inside the air-conditioned offices of the crude border-guards and the raucous scene of foul mirth, bringing into focus the tank of the water truck standing in the sweltering courtyard. Loudly crescendoing, the sound of a desperate banging on the metal walls of the tank echoes violently across the screen at the conclusion of Tawfiq Salih's film. That film, entitled *The Duped* (*al-Makhdu'un*), was made under the auspices of the Syrian Ministry of Culture where Salih had sought refuge from political pressures in Egypt, and it was both severely criticized and much lauded for the radical change it had made in the tragic and ostensibly pessimistic ending of Kanafani's textual narrative. The controversy involved aesthetic loyalties no less than ideological commitments. For example, long-devoted readers of Kanafani's novel maintained that the literary integrity of his work had been abused, if not openly violated, whereas other viewers and partisans of the film's representations found that the altered conclusion was more responsive to the new necessities of a positive and less critical image of the Palestinians' political aspirations. The question became ultimately whether it was lit-erarily and politically appropriate – for either Kanafani or Salih – to represent the three Palestinians accepting their gruesome death by suffocation with no evident attempt at struggle or resistance against their fate.

Within the terms of the novel itself, however, the situation remained decidedly ambiguous. While there is no direct or explicit evidence that the three men *did* bang on the walls of the water tank to attract attention and be rescued from their dire fate, the only indication that they *did not* bang and appeal for help is the final desperate question of the truck's driver, Abul Khaizuran: "Why didn't they knock on the sides of the tank?" According to Fadl al-Naqib's reading of the novel, however, the very question, "Why didn't they bang on the walls of the tank?" is itself an ignorant one. It ignores the historical possibilities immanent in the writer's own narrative at the same time that it serves finally to justify or legitimize the fate of the three men and exculpate others of any complicity in, or responsibility for, that fate. According to Fadl al-Naqib's interpretation of the critical scene at the border:

> there is no doubt that the three men did knock on the walls of the tank. They shouted, called for help and did everything in their power to save their lives. They did what any man would do who still clings to life. The three finally suffocated, not because they didn't bang on the walls of the tank, but because there was no one there to hear them, and even if someone did hear them, he wouldn't have taken it upon himself to help them. Nonetheless the question is a real one and in the future will become an impor-tant one in that it represents the way in which the Arabs have dealt with the [Palestinian] tragedy. We always predict a tragedy before it happens, and we are always surprised when it finally does occur. "Why didn't they bang on the walls of the truck?" will become one of the important questions in Arabic literature. (1983, pp. 44–5)

Kanafani, who himself viewed Tawfiq Salih's film at least three times in the year between its making and his own death in 1972, did not disapprove of the director's new ending. In fact, on one occasion when he watched the film in the company of his cousin, Farouq Ghandour, who was later to become the editor of his collected works, Kanafani asked him not to raise once again in the discussion following the film the futilely controversial question of the altered ending.[1]

Kanafani's "men in the sun," dispossessed and living in exile, are seeking to recover a land, a territory, a space. Kanafani, in telling their story – which is no less that of his own peregrinating itinerary – is attempting to create such a place, a space for them. Like Shahrazad, whose taletelling was the means to her own survival as well as that of all the other unmarried women of Shahriyar's kingdom, Kanafani's stories interact with historical time and plot, proposing alternative forms and outlining new narrative possibilities. They neither reproduce reality nor do they impose either the finality of an ending or the solutions of dogma. "Why didn't the men bang on the walls of the tank?" Rather than answering this question directly as it is posed first by one of the characters in his novel and reiterated again and again ever since by readers and critics, Kanafani's narrative presents a critical reinterpretation of the past at the same time as opening up interpretive possibilities affecting the historical determinations of the future.

A period of eight years had intervened between the publication of the novel and the making of the film, a lapse of time punctuated dramatically by the June War of 1967. These eight years, from 1963 to 1971, which were crucial in the emergence of an organized, independent and self-sustaining Palestinian resistance movement, became an integral part of Tawfiq Salih's film and its recreation of the novel *Men in the Sun*. The critical objection to the film on the grounds of its alleged cinematic infidelity to the textual original overlooks in the end its own active and productive engagement, not only with the novel, but also with historical circumstances and necessity. Stephen Heath (1981), in his examination of the relationship between film and ideology, observes that "no film is not a document of itself and of its actual situation in respect of the cinematic institution and of the complex social institutions of representation. Which is to say that the automatic conjunction of film and history-as-theme, as past to be shown today, the strategy for a cinema developed to recover a 'popular memory,' is an idealist abstraction, an ideal of film and an ideal of history" (p. 238). In other words, as Heath later maintains, "history is not to be recovered or expressed in cinema, is not a given; it is always to be gained in films, a political cinema to be developed in that struggle" (p. 242). Both Kanafani's novel and Tawfiq Salih's film participate in the making of Palestinian history, as theory and practice, both as archival record and document and as active forms of continued political resistance, and in conjunction with the emergence and consolidation of the armed struggle at the time. They resist together the denial to the Palestinian people of their rights to history, to self-determination, and to a land and a political and cultural identity of their own.

When Ghassan Kanafani published the novel, it was three years since he had lived and worked in Kuwait as a schoolteacher. From Kuwait he had gone to Beirut at the behest of George Habash to work on the magazine *al-Hurriya* (Freedom). Habash was engaged at the time in developing the ideology and strengthening the numbers of the Arab Nationalist Movement (ANM), which he had founded in 1963, and Kanafani became active within the circles of the emerging resistance organization. In 1963, however, the armed struggle and an independent and organized Palestinian resistance remained only a goal to which leaders such as Yasser Arafat, Salah Khalaf and Faruq al-Qaddumi of al-Fatah (al-Fatah at that time was still a clandestine society) aspired. Prior to 1964, the differing political trends in the Arab world had inhibited Palestinians, influenced by various pan-Arab ideologies, from establishing a coherent movement of their own. Then, in January 1964, the Arab League met and created the Palestine Liberation Organization (PLO), placing Ahmad Shuqairy at its head. This organization, which was to convene the Palestine National Council (PNC), was intended by the Arab governments to allow for a "docile" expression of Palestinian nationalist aims and at the same time to prevent the emergence of any independent or autonomous Palestinian resistance organization. At last, in January 1965, al-Fatah, which rejected the idea that the liberation of Palestine would be carried out by the Arab regimes, launched its first armed action against Israel, using the cover name of al-Asifa (the Storm). Already in 1964, however, the ANM had presented a program of armed struggle inside Palestine. In 1967, meanwhile, Gamal Abdel Nasser, Egypt's president and the charismatic leader of pan-Arabism, was still considered to be Palestine's savior, and most Palestinians – like the "men in the sun" – were waiting for salvation and liberation to be delivered to them.

The June War 1967, and the massive defeat of the Egyptian army, brought a bitter end to such illusions of a pan-Arab deliverance. Following the war, then, George Habash founded the more radical, Marxist-Leninist, Popular Front for the Liberation of Palestine (PFLP) of which Kanafani became a member and spokesperson. On 21 March 1968, the battle of Karamah began when Israeli troops attacked Palestinian strongholds in the hills around the Jordanian town of Karamah, just inside the border between Jordan and Israel. Informed of the impending attack several days before it was launched, the Palestinian commandos were able to muster their forces and succeeded in holding back the Israeli invaders. The battle of Karamah itself thus became legendary in the history of the nascent Palestinian resistance movement; the guerrillas, who had hitherto been regarded as outlaws and bandits, were now hailed as emergent national heroes. The movement even found that it was unable to handle the thousands of recruits who hurried to join its new fighting ranks. The Palestinian fedayeen, in withstanding the Israeli attack, had managed to do what no other Arab army had been able to accomplish. Strengthened by this victory and its increasing and intensifying operations inside Israel and the recently occupied territories of the West Bank and the Gaza Strip, al-Fatah was able to take control of the Palestine Liberation Organization at the meeting in February 1969 of the Palestine National Council. With al-Fatah's takeover, the doctrine of the "democratic secular state" as the future of Palestine was presented as the PLO's political goal and the basis of its military struggle. Salah Khalaf (Abu Iyad), one of the original members of al-Fatah, points out in his autobiography, however, that the ideal of the democratic secular state had in fact been part of al-Fatah's founding program: "From the very beginning, then, the founders of Fatah had foreseen the possibility of creating a democratic state in all Palestine in which Jews, Christians and Muslims could live in harmony as equal citizens. In the early stages, however, various political factors prevented us from making public the proposal we were to offer the Israeli Jews in 1968" (1981, p.31).

September 1970 has ever since been designated "Black September." The last weeks of that month witnessed the violent unleashing of the Jordanian government's angry hostility toward the Palestinian commandos operating inside the borders of the Hashemite kingdom. Less than a year later, in July 1971, they were attacked once again by the Jordanian army which finally succeeded in crushing once and for all the Palestinian resistance movement in Jordan. It was in that same year that Tawfiq Salih made his film of Kanafani's novel. One year later, on 9 July 1972, Kanafani, who had become an active member of Habash's PFLP and editor of its political weekly magazine *al-Hadaf* (*The Aim*), was killed in a car-bomb explosion in Beirut. Mossad, the Israeli secret service, later claimed responsibility for the assassination. Kanafani's obituary in *The Daily Star*, a Beirut English-language newspaper, read: "Ghassan was the commando who never fired a gun. His weapon was a ballpoint pen and his arena newspaper pages. And he hurt the enemy more than a column of commandos" (see Anni Kanafani, 1973). Like the children in his stories, Kanafani, writer and combatant, had indeed studied the story, across its multiple determinations, "from beginning to end."

In his 1982 article on "The Politics of Historical Interpretation," Hayden White had suggested – problematically to be sure, perhaps even cynically, given the context of the invasion of Lebanon – that the "effort of the Palestinian people to mount a politically effective response to Israeli policies entails the production of a similarly effective ideology, complete with an interpretation of their history capable of endowing it with a meaning that it has hitherto lacked" (p. 135). Kanafani's own interpretation of history, as elaborated in his narration of the story of the "men in the sun" two decades before had proposed instead the imperative of an open-ended history, a historical interpretation which would both allow for the critical question "Why didn't they knock?" and solicit self-critical answers to it. Kanafani's story, and against White's more binaristic formulation, neither purports to "serve as custodian of realism in political and social thinking," nor does it propose the vision of a

"final solution." That is to say, there is no way finally to "understand what the story meant from beginning to end." It only
happens that the "threads begin to grow clearer."

By the time, then, that Tawfiq Salih came to film *Men in the
Sun*, many of these threads had indeed "grown clearer," and the
director was able to rearticulate the events of the novel guided by
the intervening historical sequence of events. In this he differed
from Abul Khaizuran, whose "lorry moved over the sandy track
with a muted noise, while he went on thinking. He wasn't thinking in the strict sense of the term, but a series of disconnected
scenes was passing ceaselessly through his brain, incoherent and
inexplicable. He could sense exhaustion creeping through his
limbs like a straight column of ants" (pp. 54–5). *The Duped* is
the story of the emergent Palestinian resistance movement,
framed through the film's reinterpretation of the opening and
closing scenes of Ghassan Kanafani's novel. It is not simply that
"Abu Qais rested his chest on the damp ground" (p. 9), as in the
novel, but that in lowering himself to the ground he is portrayed
in the film as performing a *raka'a*, or the ritual movement of sub-
mission which is part of the Islamic prayer. In the closing scene of
the film Abul Khaizuran leaves the Palestinians on the municipal
refuse heap just inside Kuwait, the corpses of his three passengers
contorted in the resistant postures of death. Abu Qais's fist,
clenched, albeit without its wristwatch, is thrust into the air:
now become the symbol of the emergent Palestinian struggle.
Like Kanafani's novel, Tawfiq Salih's film is part of the
Palestinian movement's armed struggle against the necessity of
historical endings, a struggle against the implacability of terms
and terminations, which depends on stories and films as much as
on kalashnikovs. Like the PLO Research Center, the film and
photographic archives of the Palestine cinema organization are
part of the "struggle for history". Thus the sixth and final part of
the manifesto presented by the Arts Committee of the PFLP
adamantly supported the "training of combatants in cinematic
photography and the establishment of cadres capable of using a
camera on the battlefield beside the gun" (cited in Hul, n.d., p.
35).

The historical record of the Palestinians would be further written in crises in the decade following Tawfiq Salih's cinematic

interpretation of Kanafani's novel. The October War of 1973 was seen in the Arab world as a moral victory for the Arabs, albeit a military defeat for the Syrian and Egyptian armies. Three years later, in November 1977, Anwar al-Sadat, who had succeeded Nasser as president of Egypt, made his separate peace with Israel and concluded these negotiations with the Camp David Accords of 1979. As a result, Egypt found itself isolated from the rest of the Arab world. In June 1982, however, Israel invaded Lebanon with the announced intention not only of securing its northern borders but of destroying the political leadership of the PLO and its fighting forces in that neighboring country. Subsequent pressure from the United States and Israel on the Lebanese and Egyptian governments to "normalize" their relations with Israel had further consequences for intellectuals, writers and academics in those countries and in the Occupied Territories. The debate over "cultural cooperation with the enemy," which had been the topic of the last part of the last article that Kanafani wrote before his death in 1972, was again placed on the political and cultural agenda. In Egypt, leftist intellectuals, for example, established the journal *al-Muwagahah* (*Confrontation*) as a forum for the discussion of national culture and the "normalization of cultural relations" (see Harlow, 1986). In Israel and the Occupied Territories, the very existence of Palestinian cultural institutions, whether universities, theaters, journals or publishing houses, remained subject to harassment, closure, controversy and critical debate. Elias Khoury, a Lebanese activist, writer and critic, maintained in an interview in the newspaper *al-Nada'* upon his return from Europe to Beirut in the fall of 1982: "The critical priority as I understand it is the attempt to situate the literary text in its temporal context . . . How do you write criticism in a time of upheaval like the Arab time in Lebanon? This very upheaval is what gives to criticism a new significance, a meaning of search and acceptance of temporal emptiness and the disintegration of standards of measurement" (November 1982).

In the novels that he was to write after *Men in the Sun*, Kanafani's literary and political position evolved. In *All That's Left to You* (1966), the protagonist experiences the first impetus to resistance and armed confrontation both with his enemy and

with his own fate. *Return to Haifa* (1969) elaborates on the
ideal of a "democratic solution" to the question of Palestine, and
Um Saad, subject of the collection of stories that bears her name
(1969), achieves the realization that the Palestinian people
require the solidarity of all dispossessed peoples against the hegemonic institutions and regimes which have confiscated not only
their right to a livelihood but also their claim to a historical
existence. Already in *Men in the Sun*, however, Kanafani had
begun to map a "*contested space*" (p. xix), marked by what
Edward Said has described as the ways in which the "scene is
itself the very problem of Arabic literature and writing after
1948" (p. xxi, emphasis in original). Kanafani's critique of a
quiescent religion and capitalist ambitions is explicit in *Men in
the Sun*, and the novel can be seen to participate in what Michel
Foucault has described as the "battle for history, which is now
taking place." The very work struggles against the "will to cod-
ify, to strangle . . . the 'popular memory' and indeed to impose
thus on people an interpretive framework for the present"
(1974, p. 13).

Kanafani's work, however, engaged past peripeties no less
than present pressures, and argued with future priorities as well.

The 1936–39 Revolution in Palestine

In "The 1936–39 Revolution in Palestine: Background, Details
and Analysis" (Thawra 1936–39 fi Filastin: Khalfiat wa tafasil
wa tahlil), Kanafani proceeds according to an apparently
straightforward, at once disciplined and disciplinary, narrative
development to present the "background, details and analysis"
of the events and determinations of those three decisive years.
The essay begins with a historical setting for the uprising; this
opening is followed by a discussion of what Kanafani contends,
more controversially, were its principal agents: workers, peasants
and, within certain limitations, the intellectuals; and the reading
concludes with a report on the "revolution" (*thawra*) itself.
According to Kanafani, the Palestinian struggle had, at the time,
as it would continue to do, to contend with three mutually conflicting but interconnected issues and/or obstacles: 1. the

reactionary local leadership; 2. the Arab regimes surrounding Palestine; and 3. the Zionist–imperialist alliance (p. 45).

While the local Palestinian leadership, or indeed any other of these negative actors, may not be given an entitled site of its own in the text, Kanafani's iconoclastic critique of the roles played in the emergence and the perpetuation of the revolt by the workers, peasants and intellectuals focuses on the calculated and self-interested obstruction of the revolt (and thus the historical necessity of its ultimate collapse in 1939 on the eve of the Second World War), by the traditional leadership, including landlords, the clergy and the middle bourgeoisie – as well as on the weakness of will and the compromised organization of the left generally and the Communist Party in particular.

And while numerous causes have been cited by very different parties (see Johnson, 1982, and Swedenburg, 1995, for example) to explain the genesis and outbreak of the now historic 1936–39 revolt – whether this be the popular example of the martyred Shaykh al-Qassam or various British White Papers – it is Kanafani's argument that it was rather the violent internal contradictions, the class and religio-ethnic differences, produced by the enforced "transformation of the Palestinian agricultural economy into an industrial Jewish economy" that must be analysed if the specific contributions of the uprising to the history of popular revolution can even begin to be comprehended.

"What the story meant from beginning to end:" was the uprising spontaneous? organized? or even "theorized?" A similar query would arise again, half a century later, with the Palestinian intifada. Were the origins of that more recent history, celebrated as beginning on 9 December 1987, in fact long-standing pressures? Were they, that is, to be located instead in specifically immediate events? Or did they derive as the relentless consequences of longer-term processes of settings and precedents? On 9 December 1987, an Israeli army vehicle had crashed into a car carrying Palestinian day laborers from Gaza, killing four of them. What followed, in other words, was the "intifada." Its consequences have yet to be calculated – intifada, negotiations in Madrid, Washington DC, Oslo, the new Palestinian "authority," and now disputatious and disputed elections; the translations of hierarchical power from inside to outside, the retaking of that power in the Gaza Jericho First Agreement, and the establishment of the Palestinian Authority (a *sulta* [power] that is as often as not referred to by residents of the Occupied Territories as *salata* [salad]). Because Kanafani's analysis of the 1936–39 revolt cited just such critical vexations, its terms remain drastically relevant.

While Kanafani's essay observes the formal decorum and conventions of its genre, the analytical argument that he proposes radically transgresses the received doxa of a dominant or elite Palestinian history, exposing the orthodoxies and their proponents to historical pressures, and challenging purposively the authority of the traditional leaders, the cultural and political institutions they represent, and the inherited narratives they have come to sponsor. Like Ranajit Guha's critique of the "elite historiography of colonial India," Kanafani's analysis of the 1936–39 revolt in Palestine, by proposing a combined class and "conjunctural" reading, refuses to accept the traditional formulations of insurgency either as a "law and order problem" or as a "response to the charisma of certain elite leaders" (p. 39).

The interrogative exchange, the session of questions and answers, cited by Kanafani between a public prosecutor for the British Mandate and a Palestinian poet arrested for his rhetorical participation in a demonstration at the time stands as emblematic for the writer himself of the contention between competing narratives – and the alternative strategies, rhetorical, political and theoretical – for reconstructing resistance:

> *Prosecutor*: The reports say that you were standing above the heads of the people, with the masses behind you, shouting: O Christians, O Muslims!
> *Accused*: Yes.
> *Prosecutor*: And that you also said: Who will you leave the country for?
> *Accused*: Yes.
> *Prosecutor*: And then you said: Slaughter the Jews and the infidels.
> *Accused*: No. That would have been an infraction of the meter and the rhyme. What I said observed the rules of meter and rhyme. Poetry must speak the meaning. (p. 57)

The language of criticism, of questions and answers, like the terms and terminations of interrogations and negotiations, and no more or less than the language of poetry, would remain crucial to Kanafani's participation in the Palestinian revolution in the years before – and the decades after – his death.

Blind Languages

"Thoughts on Change and the 'Blind Language'" ("Afkar 'an al-taghyir w-'al-lugha al-'amya'") was originally presented by Ghassan Kanafani on 11 March 1968 as part of a public lecture series in Beirut that had invited major Arab writers and intellectuals to consider the impact of the June 1967 defeat on Arab society, cultural politics and critical thought. As such, Kanafani's text can be located within the context of the enormous corpus of theoretical, historical, ideological, emotional, literary and lyrical reassessments of the limited successes and multiple defeats and setbacks of recent Arab history that had emerged in the immediate aftermath of that war and that continue even today, some two decades later, to characterize much of contemporary Arab cultural production. As Faysal Darraj would point out:

> The June 1967 defeat was the most serious event in modern Arab history. Its significance and results surpassed those brought about by the establishment of Israel in 1948. Israel's establishment was an expression of the defeat of the Palestinian people and the impotence of the Arab regimes in a certain historical period when they were dependent on the colonial forces. But the June defeat was an expression of the defeat of the Arab revolution as a whole. (1989a, p. 26)

"Thoughts on Change and the 'Blind Language'," however, distinguished itself in 1968 when it was written and now again nearly thirty years later, within this particular literary history by its materially grounded critical analysis of the otherwise too prolific tendency to an unreconstructed and tyrannical fetishization of the proverbial stratagem of "self-criticism."

Ghassan Kanafani is best-known, if not exclusively so, in

English translation for his literary writings, the short stories and novels such as *Men in the Sun, Return to Haifa* and *All That's Left to You*. Consistent, then, with the international division of labor as applied to global economic development, the metropolis, in the cultural arena, has in recent years "discovered" the literary work of its former colonies. The commercial importation of the "raw materials," intellectual properties, of poetry, fiction and even drama have in turn provided the resources for the alleged theory manufactures of the West where these materials are processed and transformed into consumable commodities for an elite audience – and only later in a revision of free trade's "rules of origin" re-exported to their places of production. What is conscientiously neglected in this traffic in and redistribution of intellectual goods is the critical and theoretical contribution from the erstwhile "periphery" that would challenge a dominant paradigm of economic and cultural dependency. And while Kanafani's literary narratives, like *Men in the Sun*, themselves elaborate a rigorous critique, on the basis of class and ethnicity, of distorted social and political relationships of power, he was – and has remained – furthermore a major critic, historian, journalist and theorist of the Palestinian resistance, whose life's work was terminated in his assassination. Indeed, the last text written by Kanafani before his death and published posthumously, "On the Case of Abu Hamidu and Cultural 'Cooperation' with the Enemy," had suggested the determining outlines of a radical analysis of, first, the role of gender within the revolutionary movement and, second, the material conditions limiting the strategic relations, exchanges and negotiations between select representatives of the Israeli and Palestinian parties to the "Middle East conflict."

"Thoughts on Change and the 'Blind Language'" itself proposed a similarly critical reading of the Arab sociopolitical arena, and the essay's combined lexicon of political scientific terminology, such as "patriarchy" (*qa'ida al-'ubuwa*) and "party activism" (*hizbiyya*), and the more metaphorical terms of organicity such as "blind language" (*al-lugha al-'amya'*) and the "circulation of blood" (*al-dawra al-damawiyya*), makes manifest the necessary and critical intersection in Kanafani's work of what has often and elsewhere been dichotomized into the cultural and the political. Contained in each of these apparently disparate but theoretically interconnected key terms is Kanafani's historical focus in the essay on the "younger generations" in the Arab world and the possibilities for social and political renewal they represent. That same commitment to a younger generation also informs his fictional works where it is often the child – and, not unlike Naji al-Ali's Hanzalla, the observant "child of the camps" – who introduces the historicizing potential inherent in the dynamics of critical contradiction. In the opening pages of *Men in the Sun* (1962), for example, it was Abu Qais's son who had reminded his father of the difference between an educated critical analysis and the defeatism of religious resignation. Again, in *Return to Haifa* (1969), it would be the Palestinian child, Khaled/Dov, abandoned by his parents in their flight from Haifa in 1948 and now a recruit in the Israeli army, who instructs his parents, when they find him again in 1967 on "returning" home following the "defeat" and the opening of the borders between Israel and the now Occupied Territories. Khaled/Dov reminds Said S. and his wife Safiya of the lessons of secularism and the danger of too sectarian a definition of nationalism. So, too, the young boy in the early short story, "The Slope" (1961), had provided the liberatory example, to both his father and his teacher, of refusing the finalities of historical and narrative closure. Like Edward Said's polemical concept of "affiliation" perhaps, Kanafani's argument for the restoration of the "circulation of blood" in the Arab and Palestinian social and political corpus continues to demand a radical restructuring of the patriarchal and authoritarian ties of genealogical and hereditary filiation into the more collective, "democratic," bonds of affiliation.

The projective historical narrative of defeat and still immanent renewal traced in Kanafani's analysis in "Thoughts on Change and the 'Blind Language'" of the material and intellectual conditions of the Arab world in its immediate post-1967 phase can be further located within the larger political debates of the period, the apogee perhaps of the struggles for national liberation throughout Africa, Asia and Latin America as well as in the Middle East that marked the beginning of the end of territorial imperialism. The need stressed by Kanafani for an adequate assessment of the material and political strengths of the "enemy,"

as well as of one's own concrete possibilities within historically
determined circumstances, remained critical to the resistance
agendas of other "Third World" theorists, such as Amilcar
Cabral of Guinea Bissau and Frantz Fanon, as was also the
debate between vanguardism and popular struggle in resistance
organizations from Nicaragua and El Salvador to the Philippines
and China. Kanafani's examination of the multiple contradictions, of greater and lesser magnitude, confronting the Arab
world in the aftermath of the 1967 defeat responds critically, for
example, to Mao Zedong's 1957 statement "On the Correct
Handling of Contradictions among the People." The essay's own
insistence on the vital importance of the party, of party formation
and party activism, in creating cadres as well as a popular democratic revolution, together with the critique of an overweening
fetishization of the "leader," is not without its analogue in the
work of Antonio Gramsci on revolution, the state, the intellectual and the people, in particular its incarnations in the "modern
prince." The theoretical premises and specific historical analyses
elaborated by Kanafani in "Thoughts on Change and the 'Blind
Language'" thus firmly ground the essay in the political controversies, in the Arab world in particular but in the international
arena as well, of the time of its writing.

Read now, some thirty years later, in the period of alleged
post- (or neo-) colonialism, those same theoretical premises resonate once again, albeit within new historical configurations,
the impositions of economic imperialism, "technological under-
development," multinational capital and the "post bi-polar
world order." The promise seen by Kanafani as once offered by
Lebanon has been forfeited in the wake of civil war and the
Israeli invasion to sectarianism and the power struggles of ever
more fragmented militias and their respective sponsors, from
local warlords to international maneuverings. On a more
extended theoretical level, according to Faysal Darraj, "The
essential character of the prevailing Arab culture is not mani-
fested in political allegiance or a partisan position, but in a series
of ideological stereotypes which fight the defeat from defeated
positions" (1989a, p. 25). A new concatenation of dates has succeeded, then, to 1967 in the Arab historiographical narrative:
1970, 1973, 1977–78, 1982. From December 1987, however, the

calendric trajectory was no longer punctuated by decisive years, but projected through the continuation of the Palestinian intifada in the Occupied Territories: "in the first, second, third . . . twentieth month of the intifada" – a historical sequencing eventually conscripted by still another agenda codified by the Gaza Jericho First Agreement of 1993. The urgent theoretical issues raised by Kanafani in "Thoughts on Change and the 'Blind Language'," issues of patriarchy, party, blind language, the circulation of blood, and democracy, too, are currently being resubmitted from within occupied Palestine to the challenge of new historical developments. In an article entitled "The Intifada: Political Creativity and Popular Memory," Faysal Darraj, anticipating the renewed problem of authority (*sulta*) and in response to those challenges of theory, practice and the demands of history, had claimed that "the intifada does not deliver a theoretical speech, but is making out of its multiple practices the highest form of theoretical discourse." Darraj went on, however, to ask, "but if its practice of creative theory without articulating it, its practice of revolutionary theory, leaves to 'others' the task of translating practice into the realm of written theory, when will the practice come to write its own theory?" (1989b, pp. 40–41).

The urgency with which Ghassan Kanafani's work continues to speak to the social terms and political issues of the Arab world certainly, but in the global context as well, raises once again that other question: If Ghassan Kanafani were alive today, are there not still those who would find it necessary to assassinate him?

Naqd al-dhati/Naqd al-rifaqi: or "What will the resistance say to the people?"

If Kanafani's reading of the lexicons, slogans and rhetorics of "blind language" followed most immediately upon the disastrous defeat by Israel of the Arab armies in the June 1967 War, still another crisis for the Palestinian resistance would ensue shortly before his own death in July 1972: that of "Black September" 1970 and King Hussein's attack on the Palestinian organizations quartered in Jordan. In a series of articles published in *al-Hadaf*, as well as in *Shu'un Filastiniya*, and even in an

interview in *New Left Review*, Kanafani insistently posed the
questions for the resistance that these dire events had both immediately engaged and ultimately foretold.

Between the June 1967 War and Black September 1970, the
Palestinian resistance faced what Kanafani referred to as a "lock
and key" (*al-qafl wa-l-miftah*) historical conjuncture. According
to the critic in an article in *al-Hadaf* entitled "What Will the
Resistance Say to the People During and After the Eighth
Meeting of the National Assembly?" (13 March 1971), it was
argued that "it is possible that the key in this case could be used
to open new horizons and other levels of struggle; and it is also
possible that the opposite will happen." The very terms of the
article's title, however, indicate the parameters of the crisis: the
resistance (*al-muqawamah*) and the people (*al-jamahir*), on the
one hand, and what will one say to the other, on the other. A
divide had been opened between the leadership and its con-
stituency, a critical divide whose political issues would be
determined discursively and whose material history (during and
after/*ithna' wa ba'ad*) threatened to be decided at the forthcoming – if resolutely postponed – meeting of the Palestine National
Council (PNC). Who had the leadership been talking to? And
what had the parties to the people's fate been discussing?

1967's June War can also be referred to as the "six day war,"
emphasizing not just when but instead precisely how long (or
short) a time it had taken Israel, once it had attacked, to defeat
the Arab armies. That very difference in terminology can still, at
times, identify differing political stances and ideological dispositions towards the war and its interpretive readings. In the Arab
chronology, however, the events are also referred to as the *naksa*,
or setback, referencing at the same time the *nakba*, or catastro-
phe, of 1948, and the establishment of the State of Israel. It was
only after 1967 that the Palestine Liberation Organization –
originally formed in 1964 by the Arab League in order to absorb
the popular demands of Palestinian nationalism – achieved its
own sense of political independence and national identity. The
battle of Karamah in 1968, during which Palestinian troops sta-
tioned in Jordan succeeded in repulsing Israeli incursions across
the border, had led to substantial growth in both the numbers
and the reputation of the PLO, but the battle may just as well

have augured the beginnings of the tensions between the Palestinian resistance and Jordan's Hashemite regime, tensions that culminated in September 1970 in the massacres of thousands of Palestinians by King Hussein's army. The term itself, "Black September," refers specifically to those ten days in that month, but the actual removal of the PLO from Jordan finally took place less than a year later, following further assaults on the resistance movement and its adherents. The historical chronology established by the monthly referents of "June War" and "Black September" narrates more than a limited time line. It also articulates a concatenation of political and cultural interpretations, historical readings that Kanafani critically interrupts in his interim discussions of the infamous Rogers Plan and the series of notorious airplane hijackings by the PFLP that came between those two months and their respective years.

The "establishment of a margin (*hamish*)," and in particular a margin for "maneuvering (*munawarat*)," was what Kanafani called for in his *al-Hadaf* article of 29 August 1970 entitled "The Strategic Capitulation," a title that epitomized his definition of the terms of the Rogers Plan, presented by the United States as the latest solution to the Palestinian question and to which the Arab governments, including Jordan and Nasser's Egypt, had infamously submitted. For Kanafani, at stake were the resistance organization's conflicted relations with the people on the one hand, and with its enemies on the other. And so, too, in his article for the same journal the following week on the same topic, this time entitled "The Plot Against the Resistance," Kanafani went on to argue that the Rogers Plan itself represented an effort on the part of the imperialist powers and their ally Israel to disempower and disenfranchise the Palestinian popular struggle and, indeed, that the resistance leadership had in its turn shifted complicitously from a theory and practice of "steadfastness (*sumud*)" and "liberation (*tahrir*)" to a posture of "capitulation (*istislam*)" to the wishes of the enemy (5 September 1970). Within days of that writing, however, on 6 September 1970, the PFLP would carry out its first plane hijackings (including that in which Leila Khaled would take over a TWA flight bound from Rome for Cairo, forcing it finally to land in Syria), an occasion which Kanafani refers to as the "day of the festival of planes (*yaum mahrajan al-ta'irat*)." The celebration of the skies would be short-lived, however, as the ten days of massacre on the ground in Jordan would almost immediately ensue. The Palestinian hijackings were a necessity, nonetheless, the writer would maintain, because their own, the Palestinian, national cause had been politically hijacked by the Rogers Plan and its collaboratory drafters and signatories. The document, Kanafani argued, was based primarily on United Nations Security Council Resolution 242 passed in November 1967, a statement that had already become notorious for its designation of the Palestinians as refugees rather than as a people with their own rights to self-determination. The text of the Rogers Plan, in other words, was distinguished foremost by the complete "absence, material and spiritual, of the Palestinian people" (*al-Hadaf*, 10 October 1970). It was imperative, Kanafani insisted in the same issue, that the intellectuals work now to resist attempts on the part of Arab regimes to conscript their allegiances to their own capitulation-ism, that the writers abandon the empty slogans of the bureaucrats for a "peaceful solution," and that they coordinate in support of the "prolonged people's war" for Palestinian and Arab liberation. As Kanafani would tell an interviewer for *New Left Review* in early 1971:

> Let us recall the situation. On July 23 Nasser accepted the Rogers Plan, and a week later the Jordanian government did so too. Once again the Palestinians were put on the shelf. If you read the Arab and international press between July 23 and September 6, 1970, you will see that the Palestinian people were again being treated exactly as they were between 1948 and 1967. The Arab papers started writing about how "heroic" the Palestinians are, but also how "paralyzed" they were, and how there was no hope for these "brave heroes". (p. 268)

As for the hijackings, he went on:

> their psychological importance was much greater than their mil-itary importance, at this stage of the revolution. Now, if we had been at the final stage of the revolution, or even at the advanced first stages of the revolution and we had hijacked planes, I would

have been the first to denounce it. But in the preparatory phase of the revolution, military operations have their psychological importance. (p. 272)

Crucial to this account of hijackings – material, philosophical and political – is once again Kanafani's overriding sense of history and endings: the importance, that is, of criticism to the determinations of the narrative's development, what it might mean, after all, "from beginning to end," its reconstructions of the past as constitutive of its interpretations of the present, and contributing to the making of the vision of the future that it would sponsor. Not the exculpatory indulgences of "self-criticism" (*naqd al-dhati*), however, but the constructive, collective probings of "comrade criticism" (*naqd al-rifaqi*), are what Kanafani proposes in his article, "The Resistance Facing a Fateful Choice . . . . What Now?" (*al-Hadaf*, 2 February 1971) – if, that is, the resistance is ever to be able to "transform criticism and self-criticism into a path worthy of the revolutionary project." Or again, as he would describe his own inquiry to *New Left Review*'s interlocutors:

> In such periods of relapse, there are always divisions, exaggerations, romanticizations, tendencies to individualism and to turning the revolution into a myth and so on. These are the illnesses of the underdeveloped world, and they express themselves in a period when one is not engaged in real revolutionary work, but one is nevertheless regarded as making a revolution. (p. 277)

What indeed will the resistance say to the people – during and after the eighth meeting of the national council – about its makings of a revolution?

Ghassan Kanafani would not live to witness the subsequent consequences of his critique, but their premises were drawn out in the last article he wrote before he died in July 1972, and which was published posthumously in August 1972. In "On the Case of Abu Hamidu and the Issue of Cultural 'Cooperation' with the Enemy," Kanafani again anticipated some of those very impending consequences.

The case of Abu Hamidu, a Palestinian fighter who had just

transferred with the resistance to southern Lebanon when the movement was expelled from Jordan, and the case of "talks with the enemy": two parts to the article, two apparently disparate topics to engage the critic. But each discussion also engages the other and together they articulate the urgent concerns that Kanafani had posed, over the recent years, to his comrades in the Palestinian struggle and their international colleagues: its discursive relations, the negotiating terms, with its multiple interlocutors. In the second part of the essay, on "cultural co-operation (al-t'amal al-'alami wa-l-thaqafi)" with the enemy, the writer begins with the recognition that prior to 1972 the public position in most Arab countries had been to (pretend to) refuse such relations altogether. The issue itself is, he argues, one of the most difficult and complicated that the organization had had to face, but it was crucial that the responses be formulated nonetheless on the basis of the specific conditions of a given situation. Kanafani describes two such possibilities. First, there was the instance of a dialogue that had taken place on the BBC between two Israeli and two Palestinian students on the question of Palestine, an encounter, or confrontation (muwajahah), that Kanafani opposed. He maintained that the cultural boycott was not at all a romantic project, but rather a materially determined imperative, and that furthermore one must never underestimate the substantial resources and rhetorical power of the bourgeois media abroad and their control of the means of communication to manipulate any messages or transmissions that they might still pretend to mediate. Nonetheless, the critic does argue that there is communication to be made, with "friends," that is, "with the revolutionary movement among the Western bourgeoisies." Such friends, though, are not to be identified with a given Professor Finley, the second instance cited by Kanafani, who was an American professor at the Beirut College for Women, and whose claim to be a "friend of the Arabs" is not at all ratified by the use of "Zionist textbooks" in his classrooms. The issues raised in Kanafani's analysis, of "confrontation (muwajahah)" and "cultural invasion (al-ghazwa al-thaqafi)", would resonate again strongly following the Camp David Accords in 1978 between Egypt and Israel, and their stipulated oversight of the "normalization (tatbi'ah) of cultural relations."

Talking – another vision and version of negotiation – was ever crucial to Kanafani's critical analysis of the Palestinian question – and its possible answers. In *Return to Haifa* (1969), for example, Said and Safiyya do not talk with each other as they cross the newly drawn green line after the 1967 War to revisit their former home and search for their lost son. But they do talk with Miriam, the Jewish woman who has lived in their house since 1948 and who has adopted the child they left behind when they fled the fighting over the creation of Israel nearly two decades earlier. And no less than this "fictional" narrative, Kanafani's two literary critical studies of Palestinian resistance literature under Israeli occupation, published in 1966 and 1968, on the two temporal sides of that same June War, argue the imperative of a critical exchange between "inside" and "outside," between occupation and exile, if ever the premises for a "democratic secular state" are to be delineated.

It is, however, Abu Hamidu and his story that is given primacy of place in Kanafani's final essay that opens with the commando's name, and in which he narrates Abu Hamidu's story in the second paragraph of the text:

Perhaps the most significant of the events that we are discussing, and which must be included in their descriptive accounting, is the question of Abu Hamidu: the uproar created by the charges brought against him, charges that he had raped two young women, sisters, from the village of Hasabiya, who were then shot dead by their brother. The villagers responded to this by wanting to wipe away the shame that had covered them. Then, there was the trial by the resistance movement which sentenced the fedai Abu Hamidu to death; and in order to "make an example of him for others," determined that the execution should take place in the village square. The rest of the story (*qissa*) is well-known: the villagers were not satisfied with just the execution of Abu Hamidu, and demanded as well the withdrawal of all of the fedayin from the village and its environs. And the fedayin did indeed withdraw. And Israeli planes attacked the following afternoon, bombing both the village and the fedayin, the latter before they were able to establish their new location and camouflage it. But the Israeli planes also bombed indiscriminately the streets of

the village itself. And it is said now that Abu Hamidu was
wounded during the attack and perhaps he was among the
prison's own inmates that the Israeli bombers had deliberately
targeted. (p. 8)

What would, after all, the resistance say to the people? For
Kanafani, the issues remained compelling, the lessons clear: the
relations between the Palestinian struggle and the people it pur-
ported to represent, and the degree to which the very struggle
itself managed or not to represent in its practices the vision that
it claimed to aspire to, must be examined – and revised.

The Death of the Palestinian Bride

Two decades later, in December 1994 in Jericho, as the new
Palestinian Authority was continuing to negotiate its own legiti-
macy with the Israeli government, a recently released Palestinian
prisoner was to celebrate his marriage to the woman he had
been engaged to eight years previously when he was convicted
and sentenced for the slaying of a collaborator. On the wedding
night, however, the bride was shot and killed. Accusations were
made against the collaborator's family who, it was claimed, in
seeking revenge had missed their target, the bridegroom, and
murdered his bride instead. Her funeral was a public event,
accompanied by hundreds of mourners through the streets of
Jericho. But a few days later, following further investigation, the
bridegroom was himself in the custody of the Palestinian police,
charged with the death of the woman. He had, it seems, discovered on their wedding night that his bride was not a virgin and
had exacted his own fateful revenge.

This incident, reported but briefly in the Palestinian press at
the time, betrays in its tragically related two versions – the
defense of the national honor and the punishment of a woman's
dishonor – a larger narrative: the still contentious place and status of women within the historic gains and losses of modern
Middle Eastern polities. The contrasting narratives embedded in
the account of the death of the Palestinian bride – and revealed
in the backgrounds of Kanafani's writing (the women left behind

by the "men in the sun," the silent Safiya on her return to Haifa, and the two sisters avenged and revenged in the "case of Abu Hamidu") – are emblematic of both the contemporary contradictions that disturb her own social order and its political aspirations as well as the earlier histories of a longer East–West conflict, the issue, that is, of "cultural cooperation with the enemy."

"Why didn't they bang on the walls of the truck?" And "what will the resistance say to the people?" The issue of terms – of negotiation, of interrogation, of questions and answers – that were writ so large across Ghassan Kanafani's Palestinian writings still remains crucial to the critical elaboration of new terrains, new terminations – and new geographies of struggle.

2

Habeas Corpus: Roque Dalton and the Politics of Amnesty in El Salvador

Tribulations

Marcos: (*Grabando*) El caso es que dentro de poco se celebra el aniversario de la . . . del . . . de . . . del fallacimiento de Roberto Simpson y, pues, yo . . . yo comprendo, es decir, usted comprende . . . Claro, yo también, por supuesto . . .! O sea que los dos comprendemos! Aunque bien vistas las cosas, o como quiera que estas se vean . . .! Ay, señor! . . . Pues si, Roberto es un punto crítico para la organizición y, dada esta circunstancia, yo quisiera conocer su opinión antes de aceptar dictar la conferencia . . . Ah, bueno, disculpe, es que, por lo del aniversario que le decía, la Sorbona me ha pedido que dicte una conferencia sobre la vida y la obra de Roberto. Ese es el caso y yo . . . Pues yo no quisiera que hubiera ningún malentendido . . . Esa sería todo, comandante. En espera de su respusta: el poeta.

Marcos: (*Recording*) It's that soon the anniversary of . . . of the . . . of . . . of the death of Roberto Simpson, and so I . . . I understand, that is, you understand . . . Of course, me too . . . or rather we both understand! But seeing things, or how things might be seen . . . Yes, sir! . . . So, anyway Roberto is a critical point for the organization, and given this, I wanted to know your opinion before accepting to give the lecture . . . Ah yes, sorry, it's that, for the anniversary that I mentioned, the Sorbonne has asked me to give a lecture on the life and work of Roberto.

This is the thing and I . . . That is, I didn't want there to be any
misunderstanding . . . That's all, comandante. Waiting for your
reply. The poet.
Geovani Galeas, *La Conferencia y diálogos eternos* (1990)

Marcos, a representative of the "organization," is "the poet" in
Paris recording here a cassette to be sent to his commander,
Marcela, a guerrilla leader on the ground in this play by the
Salvadoran writer Geovani Galeas, published in Mexico in 1990.
While the names have been changed – if not to protect the innocent (or even for that matter the guilty) then at least to evidence
the persistent difficulty in coming to terms with the past – the
staged discussions represent importantly the renewed political
and cultural encounter with the 1975 death by execution of
Roque Dalton by members of his own movement, the Ejercito
Revolucionario del Pueblo (ERP). "El poeta," Marcos signs himself in his recorded communication, as pseudonym, code-name,
or even pen-name, but identifying in any case a distance, professional as well as institutional, from the recipient of his address.
That distance, the ever alleged dichotomy between academic and
activist, is fundamental to Marcela's reply to her interlocutor
concerning the proposed university lecture, and she suggests to
him that in any event – at least in the course of his presentation –
he not depart from the "literary aspect" of the topic in question.
In a later exchange, the orders to him will extend further still, to
the point of a reconsideration of Marcos's very place within the
movement's dispositions and his own answerability to the stric-
tural work of the organization's "international relations."

According to Marcela, "Clearly our military forces are at a
strategic conjuncture, requiring a strict hierarchization of tasks.
We are a revolutionary organization and we are at war," she
says, and further clarifies that position: "we are not a ministry of
culture" (p. 27). But Marcos, no less dramatically, will be visited
in Galeas's play by the specter of Roberto Simpson himself, who
brings with him very different imperatives concerning his former
comrade's anticipated academic presentation: "!Una sombra!" he
appeals. "En esto me han convertido . . . En afiche, en estatua, en
palabras, en motivo para discursos, en pretexto para chantajes
políticos . . . (A shadow . . . Into this they have transformed

me . . . into a poster, a statue, into words, a topic for discourses, into a pretext for political blackmail." And Roberto doesn't stop there, but goes on:

> Es un tema de conferencia, personaje de teatro . . . Porque un cadáver es dócil, Marcos, tan dócil como una bandera, o como trapito para limpiarse las manos . . . Y ¿Sabés? En realidad me han dejado solo . . . y tengo frío. Tengo un gran frío y estoy solo, Marcos, muy solo . . ." (It is a conference theme, a character in a play . . . Why is a corpse so docile, Marcos, docile as a banner, or like a rag for wiping one's hands . . . Do you know, in reality, they have left me alone . . . and I am cold, very cold and alone, Marcos, so alone). (p. 42)

And when Marcos then attempts to explain to his friend, as he had to Marcela, that he is writing a public lecture on his life and work, Roberto answers only, "¿Y mi muerte?" (And my death?) (pp. 44–5). What, finally, of the murder?

La Conferencia is representative, according to Matthew Carr (1994), of the "birth of a new culture" in El Salvador, but it also exposes the dilemmas and contradictions imposed by a present accounting for the deaths of the past, and excavating the grounds and premises for its future projections. Would the burial sites, for example, of the struggle's victims be located, exhumed, the remains of the martyred and the massacred examined? From the village of El Mozote in Morazán to the body dumps of La Playón, the corpses spoke to the dramatic need to review the lists of the dead, establish the roster of their assassins and reclaim the effects of their brutal and untimely demise. In El Mozote, in December 1981, an estimated thousand campesinos had been slaughtered by the elite, if infamous (and US trained) Atlacatl battalion of the Salvadoran army. Their bodies were barely buried in the town in shallow graves, although the cover-up of the mass murder extended much deeper and wider, even to Washington DC.[1] In the summer of 1994, following the 1992 Peace Accords signed in Chapultepec, Mexico, between El Salvador's ruling ARENA government and the FMLN that culminated in general elections in spring 1994, the United Nations observer force (ONUSAL), in the country to oversee these processes, revealed to Roque Dalton's family the site of the writer's burial in El Playón, following his assassination on 10 May 1975, only four days short of his fortieth birthday. Dalton's body, however, would not be reburied in the new El Salvador for, as the story went, he "had been buried barely 20 inches under the earth's surface, in a grave so shallow that [his] feet stuck out. Animals started the job of unearthing the bodies [Dalton was buried along with 'Pancho' who had been killed with him at the same time] which was finished when a judge and police summoned by townspeople picked up the . . . remains and tossed them into the trash-filled ravine of El Playón, the United Nations concluded. 'The physical recuperation of the body of Roque Dalton is not possible,' wrote Diego Garcia Sayan, UN human rights director, in a letter to the family" (Wilkinson, *Los Angeles Times*, 9 August 1994). In the Farabundo Martí National Liberation Front museum in Perquín, in Morazan province – one of the FMLN liberated zones during El Salvador's twelve-year war (or what Human Rights Watch has called a "decade of terror") – there is, however, a room dedicated to political activists and important religious figures. On one of its walls hangs the framed copy of a poem by Roque Dalton.

Appeals of *habeas corpus* – "you are to bring the body" – are writ large across the terrain of what have been Third World resistance struggles over the last half century, and no less so in El Salvador. Imprisonment, torture and assassination have been overdetermining weapons, particularly in the arsenals of governments and state apparatuses, both colonial and neocolonial, but in the hands of the guerrilla movements as well. If the representatives of ONUSAL were unable, nearly twenty years after his death, to deliver the writer-critic's body to his family, the report presented in March 1993 by the United Nations Truth Commission on its investigation into human rights abuses during the war did nonetheless insist on the very failure of the traditions of *habeas corpus* in the country's judicial practice, as well as the equally general ineffectiveness of *amparo* (a legal practice similar to *habeas corpus*, but more broadly defined at times as extending to the protection against imprisonment) in protecting fundamental individual rights (see UN Security Council, 15 September 1993, A/47/1012).

The UN Truth Commission (or Comisión de la Verdad) had been given its mandate under the terms of the 1992 Peace Accord, and its work proceeded following the principle "that the responsibility for acts of violence must be publicly recognized, that victims must be remembered and that the perpetrators must be identified" (Introduction). The report also emphasized the thesis of perpetrators' accountability for their actions. And indeed, while the great onus of responsibility for the violence of the civil war was placed in the report on the Salvadoran armed forces and their paramilitary death squads, the resistance movement was also cited for its contributions to the record of abuse against the civilian population, in actions that ranged from kidnappings and extrajudicial executions to the unwary use of landmines. Among its several recommendations, the Commission gave priority to this proposition: that those "found to be responsible for serious abuses of human rights who today hold public or military office should be removed immediately. They should also not have access to public office, or a public role, in El Salvador for at least 10 years. They should also be prohibited from ever holding any military or security responsibility" (Recommendation 1). Within days, however, of the release of the Truth Commission's report, Alfredo Cristiani, then president of El Salvador, had granted an amnesty to all those individuals whom the report had indicted. What, asked James Dunkerley a year later, "after a decade of clandestinity, death squads, raids and interrogations, is a secret?" (1994, p. 6). But because the Commission's purview covered only those violations committed between 1980 and July 1991, an account of the circumstances of the 1975 death of Roque Dalton was not to be included as part of its official findings.

In "Quito, February 1976," the Latin American writer and historian Eduardo Galeano recalled the shrouded obscurity of those circumstances – even more unclear at the time. The critic's recollections of metropolitan disinterest in and the struggle's own clandestine concealment of the execution took place in the home of a friend of Galeano: "For months no one really knew what had happened. Was it, wasn't it? The teletypes did not vibrate to tell the world about the assassination of this poet who was born in neither Paris nor New York" (1984, p. 85). And Galeano would go on to speculate in pressing irony: "We all meet death in a way that resembles us . . . I always thought that Roque would meet death roaring with laughter. I wonder if he could have" (1984, p. 86). Galeano wonders necessarily about those circumstances, because the compelling speculations themselves have been brutally interrupted: "Wouldn't the sorrow of being murdered by those who had been your comrades have been stronger? Then the bell rings. It is Humberto Vinueza, coming from Agustín Cueva's house. As soon as Ivan opens the door Humberto says, without receiving any explanation or asking anything, 'It was a dissident faction.' 'What? How?' 'Those who killed Roque Dalton. Agustín told us. In Mexico the press said . . .'" (1984, p. 86). That same year, 1976, the year that Galeano and his friends had gathered in Quito, Régis Debray, the young French philosopher who had, in his own words – the phrase that he used at his trial in a Bolivian military court following the murder of Che Guevara in 1967 – "visited" the Cuban revolution and Che's struggle in Bolivia, wrote a different tribute to his fallen friend: "Gracias, Roque . . ." Debray began and ended his essay:

Porque Roque no ha muerto. Lo han asesinado innoblemente. No es, pues, posible callar por más tiempo: sería dejarles ganar el pleito a los asesinos, entrar en su juego, asegurarles la impunidad. Diré aquí, pues, lo mínimo, en espera de un día mejor, prefieriendo pecar, por el momento, de laconismo antes que de redundancia. Roque mismo destataba demasiado el énfasis y la falso solemnidad para tolerar ahora un panegírico. Amaba demasiado el dialéctica y el diálogo . . . (Because Roque didn't die. They assassinated him ignobly. So it is no longer possible to remain silent. That would only leave the field to the assassins, to play their game, assure their impunity. So I will say the minimum now, in hopes of a better day, preferring to err as laconic rather than out of redundancy. Roque himself hated the emphatic and fake solemnity, far too much to tolerate now a panegyric. What he loved most were dialectic and dialogue). (p. 248)

Laughter, dialectic and dialogue: Roque Dalton and "Pancho" were executed on 10 May 1975, the latter charged with insurbordination and Dalton accused of being a Soviet/CIA double agent as well as of commissions of "petit-bourgeois intellectualism." In support, if hardly proof, of the first allegations, Dalton's accusers brought forward the fact of his capture and interrogation by the CIA in 1974 and a putative "confession" that same year to Sebastián Urquilla as to the political compromises he was alleged to have made under questioning. The two men's deaths, however, came at the height of a debate within the ERP concerning the relative priorities of military struggle versus popular organization. Dalton supported the imperative of grassroots work among the masses against the emphasis on the part of others in the group on the primacy of armed vanguards. Following his demise, then, those members of the organization who had shared his perspective would split to form the Fuerzas Armadas de la Resistencia Nacional (FARN), while representatives of the ERP, in an exercise in self-criticism, attempted both to explain and to exculpate their drastic decision and its still more desperate execution. The sentence against Dalton was, it was admitted, a "serious political and ideological error." Dalton, the statement went on, "should never have been executed because we could not prove that he was a traitor, any more than his petit-bourgeois positions could justify his execution." Nonetheless, it was argued, Dalton himself was "not innocent of having pushed the organization into a fratricidal struggle" (cited in Tirado, 1980, pp. 49–50). Furthermore, the ERP's explanation continued, "The execution of Dalton unleashed a rabid campaign on behalf of petit-bourgeois 'intellectualism' that little by little was transformed into the work of converting Dalton into a political banner, behind which gathered the most menial and obscure positions of inconsequential petit-bourgeois intellectualism that considered itself the theoretical head – critically and rhetorically – of Latin American revolutionary processes" (Tirado, 1980, p. 52).

Less than a decade later, however, in 1983, Comandante Ana Maria (Melida Anaya Montes) was herself executed for her own position, a similar internal contest with regard to the priority of political negotiations over continued military engagement – a death that to James Dunkerley suggested a persistent history in the Salvadoran struggle of the "dreadful consequences of penalizing dissidence with death" (1992, p. 21). Following on Ana Maria's death, Salvador Cayetano Carpio, who had been one of the most distinguished members of the resistance movement since the 1950s, committed suicide, apparently (indeed allegedly) in response to his admitted complicity in his comrade Ana Maria's execution. Finally, on 3 February 1992, the month after the signing of the Salvadoran Peace Accord, Joaquín Villalobos, then commander of the FMLN, in a speech at the swearing-in ceremony of the members of the Commission for the Consolidation of the Peace (Copaz), anticipated his own forthcoming admission of responsibility for Roque Dalton's execution: "We are aware of the fact that we made errors, that we are not infallible, and that this is the moment to humbly admit this to the nation [applause]." Going on to refer to the "bliss of telling the truth," Villalobos closed that same speech with a quotation from Roque Dalton's "Love Poem" [FBIS-LAT-92-022, 3 February 1992, p. 19]. In a radio interview several days later, Villalobos would go further still in the pursuit of such "bliss": "It would be a very terrible thing," he announced to his listeners, "if after that mistake, we didn't make minimal amends, reclaiming Roque as a national treasure and also as one of the people who describes the Salvadoran nature" (*Guardian*, 19 February 1992).

"They wanted to suppress the man in order to extinguish the idea," Régis Debray had written, "but the work remained" (1976, p. 249). And in that very work – of poetry, *testimonio*, novels and critical essays – Dalton had perhaps anticipated another horizon, against even his own encomium of the need to "pinpoint the poet more as a scrutinizer of his own time than of the future" (p. 26). Dalton, the "pobrecito poeta que era yo (poor poet that [he] was"), had lived much of his later life outside his native El Salvador – in Cuba where he had collaborated with the work of the Casa de las Americas, in Czechoslovakia where he had interviewed his compatriot Miguel Marmol, and in other European and Latin American countries, returning to his homeland, that "pulgarcito" (little thumb) of the Central American isthmus, in the early 1970s. His written corpus was both substantial and provocative – and for the most part banned in El Salvador – from the early essay "Poesia y militancia en

America Latina" (1963), or his contribution to the discussions of
La intelectual y la sociedad (1969) and the numerous collections
of poetry such as *La ventena en el rostro* (1961), *Un libro levemente odioso* (1988, edited posthumously), *Taberna y otros
lugares* (1969), and *Poemas clandestinas* (also edited posthumously), the historical monograph entitled simply *El Salvador*
(1963), the "novels" such as *Las historias prohibidas de pulgarcito* (1974) and *Probrecito poeta que era yo* (again published
posthumously), and the political prose poem also published
posthumously in Cuba which was called *Un libro rojo para
Lenin* (1986). In addition to numerous other contributions of
journalism, translation and working papers toward the planning
and practice of revolutionary struggle in the crucial decades of
the 1960s and 1970s, two of Dalton's other works instantiate the
combined critical dimensions of what Albie Sachs in South Africa
was to have called the "debate of culture" and the "culture of
debate" that so marked those years (Sachs, 1990b, p. 148). In
¿Revolución en la revolución? y la crítica de derecha (1970),
Dalton takes up – and takes a polemical part in – the theoretical
controversy that had raged since the publication of Régis
Debray's *Revolution in the Revolution?* (1968). And in *Miguel
Marmol*, published in 1971, Dalton engaged in his own testimonial debate with his senior comrade and countryman, Marmol, a
communist partisan and shoemaker by trade, who had survived
an assassination attempt in 1932 and would, in the end, outlive
Dalton by nearly two decades. Marmol died in Cuba in 1993 at
the age of eighty-eight. These two works suggest importantly
both the text and the context of Dalton's *obra*, a corpus of controversy that would survive the all-too-shallow, but just as
controversial, burial of his corpse. For all that amnesties might be
granted, such swift writs cannot prosecute an amnesia, and
Dalton's work remains decisive as much for its contributions to
defining the grounds of its own historical period as in its imperative for redefining the terms of another historical process in the
making. And as the poet had already anticipated in 1969 in
speaking to the issues of the "intellectual and society":

En la América Latina, el escritor es generalmente el *outsider*
(sobre todo en el sentido político), mientras no es asimilado por

la digestión de sistema. Independientemente determinadas
vedettes que, incorporadas a la *industria de la enajenación*,
cobran con su alto *status* social los dividiendos del régimen, el
escritor y artista latinoamericano promedio lucha en distintos
niveles contra el régimen que lo discrimina, lo humilia y lo per-
sigue: y más que el poeta y el escritor es el subversivo, el
perseguido, el preso, el torturado. Y comienza a ser el asesinado.
(In Latin America, the writer is generally the outsider [particu-
larly in a political sense] at least in so far as he has not been
assimilated by the system. Aside from those writers [vedettes]
who have sold out to the system, the average Latin American
artist and writer struggles in different ways against the regime
that discriminates, humiliates and pursues him. More even than
poet, writer, he is the subversive, the persecuted, the imprisoned
and the tortured. And now he is beginning to be the assassinated). (emphases in original, pp. 25–6)

Trials

In 1992 Joaquín Villalobos published *Una Revolución en la
Izquierda para una Revolución Democrática* (*A Revolution in
the Left for a Democratic Revolution*), the very title of which at
once betrayed and sought to restore an interrupted genealogy of
intellectual debate and revolutionary struggle. It could well be
argued that Villalobos's titular gesture contained an unwarranted
appeal to the authority of the already cross-referenced works of
Régis Debray and Roque Dalton published nearly three decades
previously: *Revolution in the Revolution?* and *¿Revolución en la
revolución? y la crítica de derecha* respectively.

Within a year of its publication in 1967, the young French
author of *Revolution in the Revolution?* was in a Bolivian prison
facing charges of conspiring with the guerrillas against the state.
The by then legendary guerrilla leader, Ernesto "Che" Guevara,
had at the same time been killed in a military ambush against his
foco in the Bolivian countryside. Questions of strategic priorities,
as well as issues of ideological commitments, were once more
critically paramount within the ranks and among the leaders of
Latin American revolutionary movements. Debray's testimony,

his "speech from the dock," at his courtmartial in Camiri, Bolivia, in 1967, identified the significance of his much debated book and its role in mustering the charges against him: "there only remains," he declared to the tribunal, "my work *Revolution in the Revolution?* which proves me, according to the prosecuting attorney, to be the 'intellectual author' of the so-called murders of March 23rd and April 10th [in which members of the Bolivian army were killed by Che's guerrillas]" (p. 36). Debray's countryman, Jean-Paul Sartre, would similarly point to the decisive role of that written work in Debray's sentence to thirty years imprisonment in his introduction to the French edition of the controversial text: "Régis Debray has been arrested by the Bolivian authorities," Sartre wrote, "not for having participated in guerrilla activities but for having written a book – *Revolution dans la revolution?* – which 'removes all brakes from guerrilla activities'" (Huberman and Sweezy, 1969, p. 11).

But if the book itself, and its subsequent interpretation by the governmental authorities, had provided critical evidence for the Bolivian state prosecutor in determining Debray's culpability and defining a thirty-year sentence against him, that very sentence in turn became a systemic part of the critically controversial readings and responses to *Revolution in the Revolution?* from its other international audience. As Joe Slovo, the South African communist, anti-apartheid militant and husband of Ruth First, would begin his critique of the book in *The African Communist*, "The passion which Régis Debray feels for the cause of the Latin American revolution cannot be questioned. The savage sentence of thirty years imposed upon him by the Bolivian regime came at the end of a trial in which he distinguished himself by a bearing in the best revolutionary traditions" (1968, p. 37). Nonetheless, Slovo goes on to ask, "Ought we, even temporarily, to be deflected from subjecting the tendencies evident in Debray's approach to the strictest scrutiny?" and concludes, "Certainly not" (p. 38). For Slovo, the "influence of theories of struggle, their adoption or rejection, is often literally a matter of life and death for thousands of militants or indeed a whole movement" (p. 38). Thus, many of the contributors to the 1968 colloquy on the book's theoretical and practical premises, organized by Leo Huberman and Paul Sweezy of *Monthly Review*, would similarly contextualize their critical remarks on the topic of "Régis Debray and the Latin American revolution" by reference to Debray's trial and sentencing. Simon Torres and Julio Aronde, for example, maintained that "[o]nly the interests of the revolutionary movement justify challenging the work of one who can hardly participate in the debate at this moment" (p. 45). Indeed, Huberman and Sweezy themselves introduced the collected discussion with the comment that "Régis Debray, as a result of a series of events which received world-wide publicity, is now serving a thirty-year sentence in a prison of United States imperialism's Bolivian neo-colony. He is there because, through his writings and actions, he threatened the rule of all Latin American oligarchies and their North American master. We salute Régis Debray and send him fraternal greetings and wishes for an early liberation."

From within the fraternal greetings and the liberatory well-wishes, however, came too the probing criticisms of, and challenges to, Debray's theses in that work. These alternative analyses argued against the primacy he attached to the guerrilla movement over the popular organizing of the masses, against the priority of countryside over city, against the limitations of Debray's historical narrative in providing adequately developed material background to his proposals; these analyses proffered also variously constructed defenses of the Party itself as still central to the elaboration of a contemporary revolutionary movement. At the same time, and together with the acknowledgements of the Frenchman's political commitment, the question was raised of his extraneous, if not extracurricular, relationship to the Latin American struggle. Both Debray's Marxist-Leninist credentials as well as his national identity were on the line. And the several critiques accordingly combined topics of both political substance and philosophical and rhetorical style. Eqbal Ahmad, for example, a Pakistani intellectual with militant experience in Algeria during the protracted struggle there against French occupation, entitled his analysis of Debray as "radical but wrong," arguing against "Debray's contention that specific conditions in any country or region are so unique as to transcend history and thus render irrelevant past revolutionary theory no less than practice" (p. 71).

Debray's thesis in *Revolution in the Revolution?* had been the counter-project to the prevailing admonition that the "Cuban Revolution can no longer be repeated in Latin America" (p. 15), and the dialogue ensued most significantly in terms of the relation of past to present, between the authority of precedents and the innovations of transformation. Thus Clea Silva, a Brazilian sociologist writing under a pen-name, objected to the alleged propensity to "substitute for creative Marxism a theory of spontaneity" (p. 23). So, too, James Petras maintained at the time that Debray had replaced "political analysis" with a "series of formulas for action" (p. 110) that were underwritten by a "mountain mystique" (p. 113) and an attendant "mistrust of the masses and ultra-voluntarism" (p. 114). The theme of the "mountain mystique" contributed to the further reading of Debray as a "romantic" (Ahmad), appealing to youth and the "enthusiasm among intellectuals" (Silva). Gordon Lewis, in turn, in commenting on Debray's assessment of the difference between revolutionary violence and repressive violence, pointed out the similarities with Fanon's "legend of the 'noble savage'" as this stereotypical ideal had been "transformed into peasant guerrilla" (p. 116). Lewis went on to identify what he termed as a "Gallic rhetoric" (p. 116) that characterized the text of *Revolution in the Revolution?*, a formulation that was reprised by Peter Worsley in his description of the text's "Gallic systematization appropriate to an Agregé de Philosophie and a product of the Ecole Normale Supérieure" (p. 126). Juan Bosch, former president of the Dominican Republic, was perhaps the most articulate in elaborating on the geopolitical divide that seemed so decisively to distance Debray's putatively speculative writing from the work of Latin American revolutionary movements. According to Bosch, Debray's language was "typically French," his work an "acute intellectual exercise" (p. 96) and, no less importantly, Debray himself, having been, "no doubt, inspired by a curiosity typical of European intellectuals, . . . decided to see with his own eyes and experience, personally, the things that he dealt with abstractly" (p. 105).

The question of the status of the Cuban revolution within the modern Latin American historical narrative (one that still preoccupies US foreign policies, even if on different terms) – a question that had so critically determined Debray's essay – the question of Cuba as neither a "golden legend" nor a reality with nothing to "do with this bold fairy tale," that question was also central to the colloquium of writers that contributed to a renewed discussion in 1969 of "the intellectual and society." Roque Dalton, René Depestre, Edmundo Desnoes, Roberto Fernández Retamar, Ambrosio Fornet and Carlos Maria Gutiérrez, each participated in this debate: what difference, they asked, did the Cuban struggle make for the experiences of other writers within and without that narrative? Debray had argued the critical consequentialities of an interrupted scenario, had insisted indeed that "failure is a springboard. As a source of theory," he had written, failure "is richer than victory: it accumulates experience and knowledge" (p. 24), and had gone on to caution the intellectuals to revise their considerations according to the decisively transformed terms of political involvement. After all, Debray wrote, the "abuse of strategy and the lack of tactics is a delightful vice, characteristic of the contemplative man" (p. 59). And there awaits, he warned, not unlike Slovo in his own critique of Debray, a drastic "penalty for a false theory" (p. 65). As Fidel Castro would himself admonish, "certain policies belong to the field of criminology" (p. 65). For the writers who participated in the colloquium, however, that same concern with narrative, with cause and effect, sequentiality, history writ both small and large and its theoretical perspectives, would have its own encomiums and provisos. For Gutiérrez, there should be no confusion between socialism and solidarity (p. 39). Fornet queried the difference between being an intellectual in a revolution and being a revolutionary (p. 43), an inquiry that was seconded by Depestre in the association of the question of "What can literature do?" with the further precision of "What can literature do in Cuba" (p. 62) . Desnoes asked after the place of "criticism within the revolution" (p. 27), a question that was pursued by Retamar concerning the larger issue of *transición*, the role, in other words, of what Gutiérrez had termed "hombres de transición," the need to be "critical cadres (*cuadros*) or consciences" (p. 107). But for Roque Dalton, "Cuando la Revolución cubana puso la industria editorial en manos del pueblo, y liquidó el pago de derecho de autor . . . estableció el destino popular y eliminado el carácter servicial-remunerable en dinera de la creación (When the Cuban revolution handed the publishing industry over to the people, and eliminated the author's copyrights, . . . the people became the owner of its own destiny who would themselves dispose of the profitability of intellectual production/creation") (pp. 12–13).

For Roque Dalton, too, Debray's *Revolution in the Revolution?* had been a veritable "bomba ideologica" (p. 21). And while referring throughout his own analysis of that work to its author as "el escritor francés," Dalton nonetheless insists on the necessity of a materialist reinstantiation of the "theoretical" as part of the practice of revolutionary struggle in Latin America. Possibly, he writes, "more than 50 per cent of the *theory* of the Latin American revolution will be at the same time a *history* of the Latin American revolution" (emphases added, p. 114). There is a crucial difference, Dalton argued, between a "'dogmatic rupture'" and a "historical exception," thereby emphasizing as well the imperatives imposed on critical constructions by the recent experiences in/with/through Cuba. Even admitting the peculiarly "Gallic" intonations of Debray's writing, Dalton went on to conclude the urgent relevance of "una nueva manera de decir las cosas" (a new way of saying things) and to maintain that Debray, whatever else and all else said and done, had "revitaliza el ensayo como género de masas" (revitalized the essay as a popular genre) (pp. 168f.).

From "revolutions in the revolution" (Debray and Dalton) to a "revolution in the left" (Villalobos) then, the critical distance would be measured from the debate on Cuba at the end of the 1960s to the revisions of the Salvadoran struggle occasioned by the Peace Accords 1992. For Villalobos, these accords were part of a "moment of rupture in universal history" (1992, p. 5), the first words of his own essay that proposed to survey that rupture. Affiliating himself and his essay with the Debray–Dalton critical alliance, Villalobos nonetheless goes on to mark his own disassociations from its prerogatives, insisting instead on the necessity to transform the traditional leftist thinking (*pensamiento de la izquierda*) of "pressure and protest" (*presión y protesta*) into that of "construction and proposal" (*construcción y propuesta*). If once Villalobos had raised the priority of militarism against

popular struggle, a priority that resulted in the execution of
Roque Dalton, he would now, in the aftermath of the peace
accords, argue the primacy of a neoliberal compromise against
the continued imperatives of popular organizing. As he himself
proverbially pointed out in *Revolución en la izquierda*, "A veces
dividen más los principios entre amigos, que los intereses entre
enemigos" (Sometimes principles divide friends more than interests do enemies) (1992, p. 59). Dalton, however, had years before
already pressed the questions on his senior comrade, Miguel
Marmol.

Testimonios

it is enough to understand, for example, what it means for a
writer and a Salvadoran militant to receive detailed information
(and to be authorized to transmit it publicly) from an eyewitness,
a survivor, of the great anti-communist massacre of 1932 in El
Salvador.
Roque Dalton, *Miguel Marmol*

In January 1932, following an aborted peasant uprising planned
in large part by the recently formed Communist Party of El
Salvador and supported by peasant organizations and trade
unions, the military and police forces of the Salvadoran government under the presidency of General Maximiliano Hernandez
Martínez massacred more than 30,000 civilians. At the time of
the *matanza*,[2] as the massacre is popularly known, Miguel
Marmol was twenty-seven years old, a shoemaker, labor organizer and member of the Communist Party. He survived the
brutal repression of 1932, and three and a half decades later, in
Prague, he told his story to his young compatriot, Roque Dalton.
Dalton, who was born three years after the *matanza*, had become
a member of the Communist Party in 1955. A militant and a
poet who won the Central American Poetry Prize in the same
year that he joined the Party, the younger Dalton would nonetheless not survive his senior colleague and interlocutor.

What then is asked for by Dalton in the "enough" that comes
from understanding what is meant by the testimony entrusted to

him by the older communist and fellow Salvadoran? Three historical narratives, at least, intersect in often conflictive ways in the collaborative work of the two men: first, there is the significance of the year and the events of 1932 for the history of El Salvador; then develops the complicated relationship of Marmol to Dalton, of Dalton to Marmol, with its contradictory implications for representing, both descriptively and prescriptively, the role of the intellectual within oppositional movements; and finally there arises the question of the emergence, consolidation and fragmentation over half a century of the Communist Party in El Salvador. *Miguel Marmol*, in other words, opens up a critically discursive site in which these combined issues of continuing crucial consequence for political and cultural resistance are raised and negotiated.

Miguel Marmol begins as Marmol's story of his nearly fifty years as a political activist, beginning with his earliest memories of childhood poverty in the village of Ilopango and provisorily concluding with union organizing in Guatemala in 1954, as personally told to Dalton for a larger reading public. The telling took place in Prague, in Czechoslovakia, and began in an expensive restaurant when a Czech journalist who had been interviewing the older man became bored and took leave of the two Salvadorans just as the "conversation became anecdotal" and "before Marmol could finish relating the adventures of his execution" (p. 34). Dalton, however, was "transported back to [his] country, the heaven-and-hell where [his] revolutionary ideals were born" (p. 34) and thus, with the plan of writing a "narrative article, a story or something along that line," Dalton, according to his own account, arranged to meet his colleague for their first working session together on 14 May 1966, his own thirty-first birthday. Questions of politics, poetry, theory and practice proliferated and the anecdotal narrative expanded until the young poet discovered that he would have to rethink his project as a book:

> I began to realize that to write about Marmol I'd have to go
> into – and not superficially – the history of the Salvadoran work-
> ers' movement and the CP of our country, and that to go into that
> I'd have to try to "dismantle" the image of the government of the

Laborite Araujo, to reconsider the government of Martinez (about which we militants of my generation have a view that begins in 1944, precisely with its overthrow), to delve into the international situation during a period of world crisis, into several decades of history. And that couldn't be done in a couple of articles. It was then that I began thinking about a book. (p. 35)

That book, *Miguel Marmol*, was to take on some of the pressing historical and political imperatives for which both Dalton and Marmol, in their critically different but reciprocal ways, lived, participated in the Salvadoran resistance struggle and eventually faced execution(s) – and, in Dalton's case, death.

Dalton refers to that book as a *testimonio* and as such it fits within the generic configurations of cultural resistance that were then emerging from the contemporary historical circumstances of anti-colonial and anti-imperialist struggles. The *testimonio*, according to John Beverley, is a "novel or novella-length narrative in book or pamphlet (i.e. printed as opposed to acoustic) form, told in the first-person by a narrator who is also the real protagonist or witness of the events he or she recounts and whose unit of narration is usually a 'life' or a significant life experience" (pp. 12–13). More important, however, than these apparently formal criteria which suggest the *testimonio*'s identification with the autobiography, are the specific historical conditions which inform the testimonial composition and determine its interventionary challenge to the dominant institutions of literature underwritten by ascendant conventions of authorship and disciplinary strictures and definitions. Crucial to the *testimonio* is the anti-authoritarian relationship between the narrator and the compiler or "activator" of the narrator-protagonist's account of the events to which she or he bears witness. This counter-hegemonic relationship in turn implicates the reader, both in the events and in their retelling. While the "intervention of this gathering and editing" is, as Beverley has pointed out, "one of the most hotly debated theoretical points in the discussion of this genre" (1989, p. 15), the collaborative nature of the project reworks the hierarchical structures of power implicit in literature as a cultural institution. Much as Shahrazad, through her appropriation of the storytelling function in *The 1001*

Nights, transformed the autocratic structures of the sultan Shahryar's rule and at the same time saved her sisters in the kingdom from her lord's despotism, so too the necessary participation of the testimonial narrator-activist in literary production historicizes and politicizes the traditional claims to an aesthetic autonomy of culture made by its institutionally sanctioned and credentialled attendants. Rather than acting as gatekeepers to the halls of learning, authors and other "professionals," often the "traditional intellectuals" in the Gramscian sense of the term, become instead the amanuenses in a new collaborative project enabling the "voices of the dispossessed" to penetrate international media circuits and information networks.

Like other *testimonios* both interrogatory and imperative, such as those by Domitila Barrios de Chungara in Bolivia (*Let Me Speak*, 1978), Rigoberta Menchu in Guatemala (*I, Rigoberta Menchu*, 1984), Leila Khaled in Palestine (*My People Shall Live*, 1973) and Elvia Alvarado in Honduras (*Don't Be Afraid, Gringo*, 1987), Miguel Marmol's public "life" or "life experience" is rendered into literary form by another participant in the *testimonio* project. Each of these narrators, as organizer and activist among their own peoples and even in international forums, has an already articulate political voice. But whereas the women titularly address their readers, Dalton's title establishes instead Marmol's nominal relationship with the author and raises the question of a different organizational principle. The *testimonio*, transgressing distinctions of discipline and genre, introduces that politically conscious, strategically developed, even militant articulation into an isolationist literary arena and collapses its self-protective defenses. Unlike other *testimonios*, however, whose narrators are, according to convention, attributed author status, *Miguel Marmol* presents itself on the title page as the work not of its protagonist Miguel Marmol, but of Roque Dalton, its *compilador* (compiler). Nor does the relationship between the two participants in the volume derive from the anthropological paradigm of ethnographer/"native informant" or the geopolitical model of metropolitan researcher/peripheral subject. Rather, the collaboration of poet-revolutionary and Party organizer, with their militancy in common, proposes a radical reordering of literary and political priorities that engages internal Party debates, historical and generational affiliations, no less than generic dispositions. Each of the participants is dramatically re-identified in the process, just as Roque Dalton insists in the conclusion to his introduction to the *testimonio*:

> Therefore, in the face of Miguel Marmol's testimony, I rejected the first trap suggested by my writing vocation: that of writing a novel based on him, or of novelizing the testimony. I quickly realized that the direct words of the witness for the prosecution were irreplaceable. Especially since what most interests us is not to portray reality, but to transform it. (p. 40)

Indeed the conventional subject-author identification of the book: Roque Dalton, *Miguel Marmol*, might well be read against convention, as Roque Dalton-Miguel Marmol, a single volume with two authors, or two protagonists and no author at all. This reordering of hierarchical distinctions is itself informed by the combined differences and shared collective commitment of the two participants.

Marmol opens his testimony, ostensibly answering a question posed to him by his interlocutor and collaborator: "You're asking me if everything I've done and experienced was already written in my destiny? Only an academic would ask that kind of question, and it makes me think of that song about 'what might have been and never was'" (p. 45). The direct address form, the immediate invocation of a partner in dialogue, establishes a profound reciprocity between Marmol and Dalton and also implicates their eventual readers in the exchange. At the same time, however, it proposes another, no less adversarial and conflicted, relationship among them that will require a mutual elaboration in the testimony to follow: "only an academic would ask that kind of question." Marmol is not an academic, he claims, but, he insists almost accusatorily, Dalton is. This distinction is more than a personal difference between the two men and it will have fundamental polemical consequences for Marmol's narration of his biography and his attendant analyses of the contested history of the Communist Party in El Salvador.

Marmol, who began his own political career as an artisan and a shoemaker, argues the importance of working-class origins for the Salvadoran Communist Party: "We're not distorting our country's history when we say our Communist Party is the child of the Salvadoran working class, since you won't find any instances, as occurred in other countries, where the CP was primarily organized in the university or among the petty bourgeois intelligentsia" (p. 140). Marmol's identification of himself, postively as an artisan and a member of the working class, and his denigration of (the role of) academics and intellectuals, is critically thematized in the course of his narrative. It figures both in his analyses of the historical conditions of the Salvadoran struggle in 1932, when he denies sounding like a professor or adacemic (p. 290) and again in his injunctions to other colleagues in the Party to fulfill the tasks assigned them by their own class positions. Discussing the case of Agustín Farabundo Martí, the early leader of the Salvadoran Communist Party who was executed by a firing squad following the 1932 massacre, Marmol criticizes, for example, the "lack of serious studies of Martí's life, which is the fault of us revolutionaries," but he goes on to assert that "within the framework of this conversation, I wouldn't dare presume to expound on the significance of el Negro Martí in our history. That's something for communists who have had time (like Dalton, for example) to go to the university to do" (p. 173).

The insistence on the "framework of [that] conversation," the dialogue between Marmol the older Party organizer and Dalton the younger university-educated poet, even as it emphasizes their shared commitments, further problematizes the collaborative relationship between the two communists. It raises, too, the contested question about the function of intellectuals within the Party's organizational apparatus and their role in the revolutionary struggle. The argument, however, is not an essentialist one and to construe it as such would be, as Gramsci has pointed out, to mistake questions of personal identity for political analysis: "The most widespread error of method seems to me that of having looked for this criterion of distinction [of intellectuals] in the intrinsic nature of intellectual activities, rather than in the ensemble of the system of relations in which these activities (and therefore the intellectual groups who personify them) have their place within the general complex of social relations" (p. 8). The distinction that Marmol repeatedly draws between the working-class artisan and the academic or intellectual functions particularly in the critical efforts to reconstruct the events leading up to the 1932 *matanza* and to analyse historically the reasons for and the contributions of the Communist Party to the failure of the peasant uprising with its disastrous aftermath of widespread death and destruction wreaked on the civilian population and on the Party's own organizational structures and capacities.

The year 1932 and the *matanza* are radically decisive not only for the historical ordering of El Salvador's recent past but for the analysis of its present conditions and for the more visionary projections of its future political trajectory. The year, so important to Salvadoran political self-analysis, is no less a part of its literary history. Its decisiveness is underscored, for example, in Dalton's poem, "All" where he writes:

> We were all born half-dead in 1932
> we survived but half-alive
> each of us with an account of thirty thousand massacred.
> ("All" in Dalton, 1984, pp. 42–3)

The year 1932 figures just as critically in Manlio Argueta's novel *One Day of Life* (1983) where Lupe, the female protagonist and principal narrator, remembers a time when the bodies of the massacred were being found almost as indiscriminately as they had been murdered; the same year structures again the narration of the present in Argueta's subsequent novel *Cuzcatlan: Where the Southern Sea Beats* (1987) which sees the contemporary death squads in El Salvador as direct descendants of General Martínez's military forces. The attempted effacement of the year 1932 from the official record of Salvadoran history is, then, a massacre of another sort: the annihilation of the historical memory, an act of amnesia and thus the obliteration of a popular contribution to articulating a vision of the future. According to Argueta, writing in the prologue to the English translation of Dalton's *Miguel Marmol*, "The insurrection of 1932 has recently ended. The massacre is repeated, and silence and terror imposed. No one dares to deal with it, to analyse it, the facts are hidden, including the newspapers in the archives of that period. But the story is kept alive by word of mouth, from ear to ear" (p. xiii). For Marmol himself, 1932 remains the point of departure and continues as the central moment of his historical narrative: "After that damned year all of us are different men and I think that from then on El Salvador is a different country. El Salvador is today, before anything else, a creation of that barbarism" (p. 305).

The focus of Marmol's testimony in its elaboration by Dalton cannot escape the relentless pressures exerted by 1932 and the narrative's very structure and retrospective sequencing are constantly coerced by the year, the events and the critical demands that these persist in making on the rendering of Marmol's life story as a Party militant: "And one thing is certain: that the communist who doesn't have the problem of '32 in his mind, cannot be a good communist, a good Salvadoran revolutionary" (pp. 317–18). As with the 1936–39 revolt in Palestine, or the Palestinian intifada in 1987, or even the Soweto uprising in South Africa in 1976, the questions and self-criticisms would proliferate. Was the Party sufficiently prepared, materially and ideologically, to lead an uprising? Had the leadership adequately estimated the ripeness or readiness of the conditions for insurrection? Was the focus on the peasantry correct? Was the urban working class ready? Were the leaders right in postponing – even for a few days – the beginning of the revolt? The continuing conflicted analysis of the events and the aftermath of 1932 divides the Salvadoran communists in particular and the left more generally among themselves, creating divisions that are decided along generational lines as well as according to ideological, partisan or sectarian positions. For Marmol, these differences function furthermore in terms of the background or previous training of the Party member and the determining effect that this necessarily has on the critique of the early leaders of the Communist Party in El Salvador, its structures and its strategies: "To throw all the blame on the communist leaders who didn't make a successful insurrection was and continues to be a prejudiced point of view, proper to reactionary or petty-bourgeois mentalities, to intellectuals isolated from reality, who, after the events, come up with the most intelligent analyses in the world that don't serve anyone to take a step forward" (p. 391).

Although Marmol may critique both the form and the substance of later, as well as much of the contemporary analysis of the circumstances and events of 1932, he nonetheless reiterates the urgent necessity of continuing the analytical enterprise. For Marmol, such a project requires that it be carried out, not through private introspection on the part of any of the surviving participants, nor in the exclusive terms of individual castigation or judgemental reproaches, but collectively, as a historically critical project integral to the very functioning of the Party's organization and its continued active operations:

> I don't think it's my job to go into a deep analysis and a whole critique on this subject. I've only wanted to put forth a series of facts for the most part unfamiliar to Salvadorans, so that they can be examined by our youngest comrades and be made use of for an analysis. I don't have the sufficient capacity or knowledge. And I don't think this is the job for any one person alone, no matter how capable, no matter how well-versed in Marxism they may be. The result of an individual analysis of a problem so complex and so deliberately confused and distorted will always be partial. We're talking about a task for a revolutionary organization, for the Party, which we communists haven't yet fulfilled. (pp. 321–2)

The furtherance of such an analysis is crucial to Marmol's record of his own participation in – and survival of – the 1932 insurrection, and the imperative of its pursuit confers on his personal *testimonio* its larger historical and political significance. Thus he goes on: "But nevertheless, I insist that it is an indispensible revolutionary task. As for me, I'm not in any way afraid of it. On the contrary, I believe that I'll only die in peace when my Party and my people demonstrate they have learned the fundamental lessons of the slaughter of '32" (p. 322).

The vocational differences between Marmol and Dalton and their political ramifications for their collective struggle, activated by Marmol in the opening lines of his *testimonio* and pursued between the rest of the lines of his account of the history of the Salvadoran Communist Party, are reiterated from an alternative perspective and based on other critical premises by Dalton in his introduction. For Dalton, theoretical training must eventually allow for the transformation of class origins into revolutionary practice. His account of Marmol's political position also speaks to the contradictions raised by his own generational and class specificities: "In accordance with the deformed structure of the working class in a country such as El Salvador – whose history is a long progression from one dependency to another – the proper class location of Marmol is ambiguous and, in any case, to conceptualize it we would need a composite definition . . . To all this has to be added that in the course of his revolutionary development, Miguel Marmol had but sporadic opportunities to engage in more or less profound, prolonged Marxist studies" (p. 25). Dalton goes on in his reading of Marmol's autobiographical and ideological positioning: "It is clear that the level of education received by one means or another didn't diminish in any appreciable way his, I repeat, almost exclusively practical revolutionary nature. Even, let's say once and for all, a relatively *empirical* nature" (p. 26).

The critical differences between the two Salvadoran communists, and the political distances that these produce, are historical as well as class-based. Marmol in turn insists, even if at times with the nostalgia that comes of retrospection and a consciousness of the historical limitations of his own seniority, on the active agency of history in the formation of the Party and its cadres. "We were truly beginners," he recalls, "beginners in 1930, which isn't the same as being beginners in these modern times, now when there's so much experience within the grasp of revolutionary youth" (p. 197). Nonetheless, with his *testimonio* now almost complete and thus too his critique, Marmol returns to the historical continuity of these successive beginnings which narrate the solidarity between himself and the younger poet: "We began," he says, "as leaders during a historical stage that has not ended" (p. 466). But even while emphasizing the constitutive effects of history and chronology, the difference that their generations make, Marmol refuses to overlook what he sees as the originating class position of his testimonial colleague and Salvadoran communist compatriot.

The implicit analysis that Marmol elaborates throughout his *testimonio* about his interlocutor's theoretical position is explicitly rendered posthumously – and self-critically, the effect perhaps of the experience of the *testimonio* – in an interview in 1986 with the English translators of *Miguel Marmol*: "Roque," Marmol tells them, "had his conceptions of the past and I had mine. Roque was an intellectual of petty-bourgeois origin. An intellectual comrade is always more radical and extreme than a worker" (p. 492). Dalton himself, however, had continued to assume in radically critical ways in his writing the burden of class as determined by his own social background. In *Poetry and Militancy in Latin America*, the poet attempted to theorize the political contradictions posed by the "personal circum-stances in which [he] engage[s] in creative work": his "long and deep bourgeois formative period" and the "long communist militancy . . . held to for so many years now" (p. 10). The bur-dens of class are to be understood historically, not essentially or even literarily, according to Dalton, and it is less his own per-sonal identity that is at stake here than the Gramscian "complex of social relations." "Now then," he writes, "what I cannot do . . . is cross out the present effects [of the past] with the stroke of a pen" (Dalton, 1981, p. 11). His role as writer, militant and revolutionary is rather to alter the very definition of poetry:

> Poetry
> pardon me for having helped you understand
> that you are not made of words alone.
> ("Ars Poetica 1974" in Dalton, 1984, p. 58)

And his role as a revolutionary poet is to "transform reality" – and the very nature of the poet:

> That was when he began writing on the walls
> in his own handwriting
> on fences and buildings
> and on the giant billboards.
> The change was no small thing
> quite the contrary
> in the beginning
> he fell into a deep creative slump.

It's just that sonnets don't look good on walls
and phrases he was mad about before, like
"oh abysmal sandalwood, honey of moss"
looked like a big joke on peeling walls.
("History of a Poetic" in Dalton, 1984, p. 79)

Marmol's personal itinerary, as he reports it to Roque Dalton for publication, spans a historical period of half a century. The focus or emphasis of the Dalton–Marmol testimonial, however, remains that of the "political" over the "personal" in terms which too often occlude issues of gender and the need for the Party to participate in a social and political restructuring of the traditional society and its attendant gender roles. In Marmol's analysis, this traditionalism maintains its hold despite the competing historical pressures for change from both progressive and reactionary forces. Marmol's account of his relationship with his wife, in particular, as well as with other women whom he encountered on his revolutionary way, suggests some of the problematic and contradictory parameters of his critique of women's growing influence in political activity and within the Party, especially as he confronted this structural change following his release from prison. A reading of *Miguel Marmol* against the grain of his own biases and in the context provided by the *testimonios* of contemporary women activists such as Bolivian Domitila Barrios de Chungara, Nicaraguan Doris Tijerino, Honduran Elvia Alvarado and Guatemalan Rigoberta Menchu might well in turn further the possibilities for (self-)critical social and political analysis already opened up in the collaboration between Dalton and Marmol.

Rather than critically addressing the complications in his personal life caused by his political activity, Marmol instead dramatically counterpoints the significant events of his biography with the electoral and governmental history of El Salvador on the one hand, its center wrought asunder by the repressive rule of General Martínez from 1932 to 1944, and, on the other, with his growing affiliation with international communism, a connection first adumbrated in his trip to the Soviet Union in 1930 as a Salvadoran delegate to the World Congress of Red Trade Unions (PROFINTERN). That journey, which took

Marmol by ship with Yugoslavs, Germans and other Europeans across the Atlantic and brought him together with other Latin American communists gathered in the Soviet Union, resulted in an evolving internationalist consciousness and a consolidation of his own Central American commitments. It also served to establish his public identity as a communist. Marmol's brief internment in Cuba *en route* back to El Salvador initiated him into the experience of prison and political detention which were to continue through subsequent years in El Salvador as well as in Guatemala and were to punctuate his alternating periods of active labor organizing and clandestine Party work. Miguel Marmol is, according to Manlio Argueta, a "living document" (in Dalton, 1987, p. xvii), and *Miguel Marmol*, in the words of Margaret Randall, is one of those "books that are records," the "books without which the understanding of a particular time or place would not be complete" (in Dalton, 1987, p. ix). And for the poet and *compilador* of Marmol's testimony, Roque Dalton himself, who, like Marmol, sees the year 1932 as a constitutive date in Salvadoran history, "no one can inform us better about a massacre than the survivors" (Dalton, 1987, pp. 38–9).

But Roque Dalton did not ultimately survive the debates over armed struggle and militarism in the Central American context within his own political organization, debates that had found another kind of forum in the Dalton–Marmol *testimonio*. As Marmol himself had maintained a decade earlier in the last pages of his *testimonio* to Dalton and speaking of his own premature experience of posthumous celebration, "my best memories are of the moments that followed the imminent danger of death, those moments when you realize you've been reborn" (p. 482). Those memories were not vouchsafed by Roque Dalton, but by Marmol's life, the "living document," which is, as Eduardo Galeano had described it, a series of "resurrections" (Galeano, 1987), twelve in all, the most spectacular of which remains, once and for ever, the "resurrection" from his own execution in 1932 by General Martínez's firing squad.

Roque Dalton and Miguel Marmol shared finally in the experience of death as they had shared in the recreation of historical life through the *testimonio*. Their mutual and unrelenting

concern with a political analysis of that life at the expense even
of their personal identities animates the *testimonio* and continues after the fact to rework the genre itself. Throughout his
narration Marmol insists on reconstructing his personal history
as a political analysis. "You see," he told Dalton and his readers, "I don't like to dwell so much on this aspect of the
persecutions [the difficulties of family life], because this isn't an
adventure story, but simply notes of my most general recollections in the hope that they will maybe be of some use to today's
young revolutionaries. And because I realize that true revolutionaries never like to dwell too much on their misfortunes" (p.
157). In this demand for an uncompromising political analysis,
Marmol is reciprocated by his collaborator: "to study this [psy-
chology] I would need to have more than a layman's knowledge
of ethnology and psychology. And then there would be too
much about a very complex area that I prefer to maintain in the
narration simply as shading, at a level that won't disturb the
essentially political intentions of comrade Marmol's deposition
and of my elaborative work" (p. 30). Until, that is, Marmol
finally demands of Dalton:

> You ask who am I to talk this way, like I'm giving a lesson to the
> whole world? Well, simply and humbly, one old communist
> among millions of communists, who's risked his skin, and not
> just once, for the revolution, for the communist movement, and
> who's not talking at the moment for philosophers, for deep intel-
> lectuals, but only and exclusively for everyday revolutionaries,
> plain and simple. (p. 475)

It is that question, posed by Marmol the Party militant, and
Dalton's answer, as revolutionary poet, through their shared
work in the *testimonio* itself, that distinguish *Miguel Marmol* not
only as *testimonio*, as historical genre challenging the institutions
of literature, but as political analysis challenging the course of
history and the reductivist attempts to reappropriate its analysis
according to what Dalton would later dismiss as "crock logic":

> Criticism of the Soviet Union
> can only be made by one who is anti-Soviet.

Criticism of China
can only be made by one who is anti-China.

Criticism of the Salvadoran Communist Party
can only be made by an agent of the CIA.

Self-criticism is equivalent to suicide.
("Crock Logic" in Dalton, 1984, p. 67)

Is it enough, in the end, just to understand . . .?

Transitions

Lo mejor, pese a todo, es que Roque no ha podido ignorado.
Culturalmente hablando, es clave. Justamente por haber sido un
intelectual proscrito, asesinado por causa de sus ideas, es capaz de
poner a prueba la sinceridad de cualquier proyecto cultural.
(Despite it all, the best thing is that Roque could not, can not, be
ignored. Culturally speaking, he is key. Precisely for having been
a proscribed intellectual, assassinated because of his ideas, he is
capable of putting to proof the sincerity of any cultural project
whatsoever.)
Miguel Huezo Mixco, "Muchachos: matad a Roque" (1993)

En un contexto de guerra civil, la natural toma de posición de los
intelectuales con uno u otro bando los transformó de imediato en
objetivo militar.
(In the context of civil war, the natural taking by intellectuals of
a position with one or another group immediately transforms
them into a military objective.)
Horacio Castellanos Moya, "Una tumba para Roque Dalton"
(1992)

In spring 1995, the new Salvadoran parliament was debating
the issue of the death penalty: that is, whether or not it should be
implemented as part of the legal practices of the new El Salvador
(Proceso, p. 659). At just the same time, in early June, the constitutional commission in South Africa determined finally to

abolish the death penalty altogether and remove it from the penal
books and legal codes. Meanwhile, in Pennsylvania, recently
elected Governor Tom Ridge had signed the death warrant of
Mumia Abu-Jamal and set his execution for two and a half
months later, on 17 August 1995. Abu-Jamal, a former Black
Panther, journalist and writer, had been convicted – in the course
of a much contested and highly problematic trial – for the 1981
slaying of a Philadelphia police officer. According to Amnesty
International's 1995 report on the topic, half of the world's
nations have, either *de jure* or *de facto*, eliminated the death
penalty from their roster of recriminations and retributions. Its
persistence – or renewal – in countries under construction and/or
reconstruction (and from the United States to El Salvador and
South Africa) perhaps identifies a marker of their relation to
their respective pasts and the anticipation of the peripeties of
their future development. And even as El Salvador determined
officially to retain the death penalty as part of its penal and judicial practices – consistent, it might be argued, with its long
history of death squads, from the 1932 *matanza* to such quasi-
official organizations as that run throughout the late 1970s and
1980s by Roberto D'Aubisson – in 1995 newly mobilized groups
like the "Black Shadow" had begun to assume for themselves the
task of policing what had come to be recognized, both popularly
and in official parlance, as a new lawlessness in the streets, even
carried to the point of assaulting members of the Supreme Court
who seemed to have promised a new law and order for the country (see Proceso, 661, and Flor del Izote report, 6, 29 (1995)) in
the wake of the Peace Accords and as part of what was being
called *la transición*.

Among the "political suicides in Latin America," by contrast,
described by James Dunkerley, is that of "Marcial" in April 1983
in Nicaragua. "Marcial," or Salvador Cayetano Carpio, is
reputed to have been responsible for the execution of his FMLN
comrade, Comandante Ana María, that same month, and when
confronted with these allegations, chose his own death by way of
their acknowledgement. According to Dunkerley (and other
readers of the drama), Cayetano Carpio had argued for continued militancy and against Ana María, maintaining in the
movement's internal debates that "negotiations with the

government were an absolutely subordinate feature of revolutionary strategy" (1992, p. 22). That death sentence, against Ana María, like Roque Dalton's eight years before, would also again come between Régis Debray and his Central American comrades:

> Thus in April 1983, when Debray learned of the murder in Managua of Ana María, one of the FMLN's leading figures, followed by the suicide of the legendary Cayetano Carpio, also in the Nicaraguan capital, he was furious at the Salvadorans and at himself for trusting in their capacity for peaceful resolution of internal conflicts. These feelings burst out during a strained and emotional dinner in Paris at his overcrowded apartment on the Rue Notre Dame des Champs with Salvador Samayoa, the Salvadorean guerrilla he probably knew best and respected most. He also happened to be a member of the same organization Carpio and Ana María belonged to (Castañeda, 1993, p. 131).

That same history of the death sentence in El Salvador provides too the basis for the 1989 novel by Horacio Castellanos Moya, *La diáspora* (1989). Set among the exiled Salvadoran community in Mexico in late 1983, following the FMLN directorate's accounting for the two deaths earlier in the year, the novel introduces a series of principal characters, each of whom represents a particular perspective towards – and within – that account. The narrative begins with the arrival in Mexico City of one Juan Carlos, a partisan who had recently resigned his position with the financial section of the FMLN in Managua and who now plans to seek political refuge in Canada. Indeed, Juan Carlos, following the deaths of Ana María and Marcial and the organization's accounting, has broken (*tronar*) with the movement. His own explanations of that break become crucial to his finding his way to another life. He must, for example, tell his story convincingly to Rita, the representative at the United Nations High Commission for Refugees (UNHCR) who will facilitate his new status as political refugee:

> Mirá, yo salí de El Salvador en 1980, después de la huelga general de agosto. Colaboraba con el Frente Universitario y los militares

ya me tenían cuadriculado. Enfrenté dos opciones: o me iba del
país o pasaba a la clandestinidad. Desgraciadamente, nunca he
sido hombre de armas. Me fui a Managua y desde entonces
empecé a desempeñarme en el trabajo de solidaridad. Pero hace
un par de meses troné. No puedo regresar a El Salvador y en
Nicaragua la situación es sumamente difícil. Así que decidí venir
a México, con la intención de irme como refugiado a Canada.
Esa es en síntesis mi historia. Necesito que vos me ayudés a con-
sequir la calidad de refugiado y que, si es posible, me recomendés
con la gente de la embajada de Canada. (Look, I left El Salvador
in 1980, after the general strike in August. I worked with the
Front at the university and the military had their eye on me. I had
two options: either leave the country, or go underground. But I
have never been a man of arms, so I left Managua, and since then
I have gotten involved in solidarity work. A few months ago I
broke. I couldn't go back to El Salvador and in Nicaragua the situation was extremely difficult. So I decided to come to Mexico so
I could go as a refugee to Canada. That, in sum, is my history. I
need you to help me get refugee status and, if possible, recom-
mend me to the people at the Canadian embassy.) (p. 29)

But when Rita next asks him to elaborate on the reasons for his
break with the movement, "*Y por qué tronaste?*", Juan Carlos
answers only that it would be a "long story" (*cuento largo*) (p.
30). Later, however, drowsing over a novel by Milan Kundera in
the Mexico City living room of his friend Carmen, he imagines
that very story now as a novel in its own right: "Lo que sí valía
la pena contar era la forma en que se habían aniquilado entre sí
los dos máximos comandantes revolucionarios; aunque para eso
se necesitaba una pluma genial (What was really worth describing was the way that they had annihilated the two revolutionary
commanders, but for that you would have to be a genius") (p.
41). Later still, Juan Carlos would provide more, if no less
ambivalent, analysis for Rita:

Difícil saber la verdad. Circulaban muchos chismes, versiones
estrafalarias. Lo cierto era que había una lucha de poder al inte-
rio del Partido. A Juan Carlos le parecía que los puntos claves de
los cuales se manifestaba esa pugna eran dos: la unidad con las

demás organizaciones revolucionarios salvadoreños y la eventual negociación. (It's hard to know the truth. There are a lot of
rumors circulating, extravagant versions. For sure there was a
power struggle inside the Party. To Juan Carlos it seems that
there were two key points: unity with other Salvadoran revolutionary organizations and eventual negotiations.) (p. 51)

Finally, Juan Carlos will blurt out the whole story to his
unnamed abductors – and surprise himself in so doing with his
new-found narrative capacities: "Se sorprendió de la facilidad
con que hablaba. Años atrás se consideraba preparado incluso
para resistir las peores torturas antes de soltar una palabra (I was
surprised at the ease with which I talked. Years ago I thought
myself prepared to resist the worst tortures before uttering a single word") (p. 63).

Besides Juan Carlos, there is also Quique, representing the
militant alternative to the other's critical questioning, and who
has just been summoned by the movement to return to the moun-
tains and armed combat. For Quique, the ideological debate is of
limited interest except for its implicit conditioning of the continuation of the armed struggle. Jorge Kraus, by contrast, is a
famous Argentinian journalist, who has written books about the
revolutions in Angola, Ethiopia and Nicaragua, and who sees in
the story of "Marcial y Ana María" the opportunity for a "best
seller," written according to the "técnica de la novela policíaca"
(p. 136). Until now, however, Kraus "sólo había escrito sobre
revoluciones triunfantes, en las que la seguridad del reportero
estaba garantizada (had written only about triumphant revolutions, in which the security of the reporter was guaranteed") (p.
127). Finally, Gabriel, who had been Juan Carlos's university
professor in San Salvador and who now teaches at the UNAM in
Mexico City, is, at long last, completing his unfinished doctoral
thesis – on the subject of Roque Dalton:

A diferencia del caso de Ana María y Marcial, hasta la fecha no
se ha capturado ni juzgado a nadie por el asesinato de Dalton.
Tampoco se han revelado públicamente los nombres de los
autores intelectuales y materiales del crimen, ni la forma en que
fue ultimado.

Los restos de Ana María reposan en una plaza de Managua que lleva el nombre de la dirigente; Carpio fue enterrado en un sitio de Nicaragua conocido únicamente por su mujer, algunos colaboradores cercanos, la jefatura sandinista y la dirección de las FPL; el lugar donde se pudrió el cuerpos de Dalton es mantenido como férreo secreto por los jefes del ERP.

(Unlike in the case of Ana Maria and Marcial, until now no one has been captured or judged for the assassination of Dalton. Nor has there been any public revelation of either the intellectual or material authors of the crime, nor even the way in which it was carried out.

The remains of Ana Maria are in a public square in Managua that bears the name of the leader; Carpio was buried in a place in Nicaragua known only to his wife, a few close comrades, the Sandinista leadership and the directorate of the FPL; but where Dalton's body lies is kept very secret by the ERP leaders.) (p. 142)

Those details, of death and interment, nonetheless, would become at least partially known – and no less critical to the cultural and political practices of El Salvador's *transición*. And *La diáspora*'s author would, in his subsequent study of "cultura y transición en El Salvador," discreetly defer to them in citing the author of Dalton's demise in a footnote whose small print is emblazoned across the rest of the text: "Sería saludable que Joaquín Villalobos aclarara cuál fue su participación en el complot que culminó con la muerte des poeta Roque Dalton, a fin de que sus opiniones culturales sean mejor valoradas (It would be healthy if Joaquin Villalobos would clarify just what was his participation in the plot that ended in the murder of the poet Roque Dalton, so that his cultural opinions would have more merit") (p. 46n).

In the collection of essays, dating from 1990 to 1992, that make up *Recuento de incertidumbres: Cultura y transición en El Salvador*, Horacio Castellanos Moya (who in one of those essays identifies himself as a Salvadoran writer without any party affiliations) argues that the *cultura de la guerra* that had so drastically characterized that country's political and cultural life over the last decade of civil war must undergo equally drastic changes if it is eventually to become a *cultura de la democracia*.

In other words, the criteria of the former – ideologization, polarization, militarization – demand now, he maintains, their own determined reversal: de-ideologization, de-polarization and de-militarization. For Castellanos Moya, such pressures of political positioning had once left only too few critical alternatives to writers and intellectuals: "El alineamiento, el silencio o el exilio constituyeron las únicas opciones. La osadía de ejercer la critica del poder desde posiciones no partidistas implicaba la muerte: el asesinato de los sacerdotes jesuitas, en noviembre de 1989, es un ejemplo de este situación extrema (The party line, silence, or exile were the only options. To dare to criticize power from non-party positions meant death: the assassination of the Jesuits in November 1989 is an example of this extreme situation") (p. 58). And Dalton, or Ana María and Marcial?

The "derecha a la disensión," the right to dissent, called for here is just as differently historicized by another Salvadoran poet, writer and reader of the *transición*, Miguel Huezo Mixco, who for his part had long worked within the ranks of the FPL. According to Huezo Mixco, and in contrast to Castellanos Moya, Salvadoran literary history has been distinguished by combined continuities and disruptions, creating a significant "temática guerra-paz" (1993), such that the "cultura de la guerra" is itself identified as the "cultura de la transición." And still again, for Yvon Grenier, "[l]a transición política en El Salvador ha sido un estado casí permanente en este siglo (the political transition in El Salvador has been a nearly permanent situation throughout this century") (1992, p. 9). Grenier goes on to describe the effect of the peace accords on the current transition process, the question of amnesty and amnesia: "los acuerdos de paz dicen: tu enemigo es ahora tu adversario, y cuenta las cabezas en vez de cortarlas (the peace accords say: your enemy is now your adversary, and you count heads instead of chopping them off") (p. 9). As Petras and Morley (1992) would describe the larger politics of "transition," and anticipating the coming contradictions of El Salvador's *transición*:

> In the Third World, the Western-financed state-terrorist regimes (Argentina, Uruguay, Chile, Indonesia, Zaire [ex-Congo], Guatemala, etc.) exterminated a whole generation of Marxist

intellectuals and activists. They have been replaced by Western-funded "institutional intellectuals" who are more "open" to the notions of market based development and "nonclass" democracy. In the case of radical states like Cuba, Vietnam, Nicaragua, Mozambique and Angola, either terrorist wars waged by Western-backed surrogates have destroyed their productive base or global economic embargoes have served the same end, forcing them to seek economic and ideological compromises on terms favorable to the capitalist countries. These shifts in the South and East have, in turn, limited the options available to ongoing Third World liberation movements (e.g. the FMLN in El Salvador), creating pressures for accommodations with the reactionary pro-Western regimes (pp. 153–5).

In other words, perhaps not only writers but revolutions as well were martyred in the transition from interrogation and assassination to electoral participation.

Habeas corpus and the penalties of death/amnesia and amnesty: Roque Dalton's life and work, his corpse and his corpus, remain indeed, as Miguel Huezo Mixco has described, "key" (*clave*) to the determinations of transition.

3

After the Fact: Ruth First and the Politics of Dissent in South Africa

Then August '64 I was arrested, yes. It was a Sunday morning when they took me. They interrogated me, it was almost a whole day. It's early in the morning, I think they picked me up round-about eight o'clock, and I was there in that room for almost a whole day until the evening. The Special Branch said: I don't want to know what you did. I want to know something that we don't know. And I didn't know anything, you see. So he gave me a big file, you know everybody's pictures, and: Who's this? Well I know this is Ruth First. What did she do? I don't know . . . she was a journalist, she was taking photographs and she was writing. Don't tell me nonsense – you know rude – don't talk shit to me! Tell me the real thing!
Joyce Moodley in Bernstein, *The Rift: The Exile Experience of South Africans* (1994)

Writing Under Cover

In *Learning from Robben Island* (1991), a collection of study papers originally produced for distribution among the political prisoners on Robben Island, Govan Mbeki includes a detailed instructional essay, "Notes on Leafletting and Pamphleteering." That essay is especially concerned with identifying the "role of the written word in spreading ideas" (p. 88) and, more particularly still, with "examining the best manner in which an *outlawed* ANC can set about the task of carrying its message to the masses of the people, whom it seeks to lead, in order to achieve its goals" (p. 88, emphasis added). With the banning of the ANC by the South African government in 1963, the material conditions of communication, political education and mass mobilization had been radically altered. Mbeki himself had been arrested, together with other leaders of the newly armed movement, in the raid on the Rivonia farmhouse in July 1963. He was eventually sentenced to life imprisonment on Robben Island. *Learning from Robben Island* was published in 1991, following the prisoner's release in 1987 on "compassionate grounds" because of old age and ill health. Mbeki's release, however, also provided a kind of "test case" for the transitional initiatives that would be undertaken by then President F. W. De Klerk toward negotiating a new order for South Africa with apartheid's historic opponents. The collection includes, in addition to the description of leafletting and pamphleteering, essays and study sections on South Africa's economic history, Afrikaner capitalism and, importantly, an analysis of the means and ends to "good organization" as the "key to success." It opens, however, with a "memoriam" to Ruth First, who had been assassinated by a parcel bomb in Maputo in 1982.

Mbeki had in part prepared for his eventual role in the ANC leadership, a role for which he would serve twenty-seven years of a life sentence, as an economic historian. More specifically, as he was described by Ruth First, Mbeki was "recognized widely in South Africa as an expert on the Transkei and on rural and agrarian problems" (*South West Africa*, Preface, 1963, p. 9). His first book, *South Africa: The Peasants' Revolt* (1964), which First edited and to which she wrote the preface, was published only afterwards, during his first year of imprisonment. It had had, as First notes, "a painful birth." There had been no "seclusion of a study or a library, the facilities for patient interviews and field work" to assist the writer's research or to provide the endorsements of the standard criteria of conventional scholarship. Instead, the volume was composed – not unlike the leaflets and pamphlets of which Mbeki would later make an account – in township kitchens in Port Elizabeth, "interrupted by police raids," and later on "rolls of toilet paper," when the author was serving a two-month period of solitary confinement (p. 9). First goes on to describe further the book's difficult genesis, a political economic analysis which had begun as an ANC manual: in prison, "[w]ithout reference material he began again to write the book on the Bantustans, and when he was discharged from the trial and the rolls of paper were retrieved from the prison, two manuscripts lay side by side. The one was the earlier form, written largely before the banning of the African National Congress and taking the peasant story up to 1960; the second was an improved version of the first, taking the story two years later." First's editorial task, then, was to "reconcile the two versions and edit the final form of the manuscript" (p. 10). Even that work, however, as she recalls, had to be done "under cover" since both author and editor had been placed on the "list of persons banned from communicating with other banned persons" (p. 11).

South Africa: The Peasants' Revolt was published in London in 1964 in Penguin's African Library series and exemplifies the peripeties of writing on the run – and publication in exile. The series was begun by Ronald Segal, himself a South African exile who had been obliged to flee the country once the authorities had identified him as the person who had assisted Oliver Tambo in his own abrupt escape across the border to Bechuanaland when the banning of the ANC was announced in 1963. That same year, Penguin's African Library also published Ruth First's first book, *South West Africa*, a political history of that similarly contested region. Much as she had described the "painful birth" of Mbeki's study, First introduces her own volume by narrating the obstacles posed to her field research by political circumstances and historical exigencies:

'What exactly do you think you're doing?' the Archivist in Windhoek demanded, calling me into his office. 'Collecting material for a book,' I said. He could stop me, he said aggressively. We argued the toss; he produced the Archives Act, and then compromised. I could work there, but he would decide what material I could not see. From the reports on the table he withdrew all those dating from the end of 1946.

That was the year South Africa rejected the United Nations

Organization's request to put the mandate of South West Africa
under international trusteeship; she has defied the world body
ever since. South West Africa is South Africa's property: tres-
passers will be prosecuted. (*South West Africa*, 1963, p. 11)

First goes on, and perhaps even disingenuously, but still confut-
ing the conflation of writers and invaders posed so violently by
South Africa's censors and overseers, and their librarians across
the border in South West Africa: "I was no invading force," she
writes, "only a journalist bent on collecting the facts and feeling
of the South West African situation" (p. 11). Her work route
nonetheless followed a necessarily "devious" trajectory, covering
her tracks and giving new twists to the traditions of research,
interview and archival investigation, for the security forces'
"scrutiny never faltered: the trail to the dry-cleaner and the shoemaker, the skulking next to the phone booth, both ends of the
road and every exit of the hotel patrolled, detectives following
me to the airport, to the post office to buy stamps, watching me
at breakfast, interviewing people I had seen – 'What does she
want from you?'" (p. 13).

What was at stake, both in the "painful birth" of *The
Peasants' Revolt* and in the academic inquiries preliminary to the
composition of *South West Africa*, was not only a "police state
in operation" (p. 13), but the very enforcement of genre – plot,
setting and character, no less than authorship and eventual edi-
torship and publication – by contested material conditions and
conflicting political imperatives. Both production and distribution were itineraries that were challenged at multiple turns and
on myriad levels by representatives of the state security apparatus. As Mbeki would describe the task of leafletting:

Even in the days when the ANC operated legally, the effective
distribution of leaflets was always a taxing task. Under conditions of illegality the distribution of every series requires careful
planning. Every leaflet ends thus: Issued by – The ANC
(Bonteheuwel/Langa/Tembisa, as the case may be). If a distribu-
tor is caught red-handed he is immediately arrested. The police
will want to obtain as much information as possible about the
chain of command. This knowledge is more important to them

than obtaining a conviction against one individual. In planning distribution it is important that the chain is broken at occasional intervals so that a person who is caught can give information up to a point simply because he genuinely does not know beyond this point. (*Learning from Robben Island*, 1991, pp. 98–9)

The subsequent work of librarians, archivists and researchers must in its turn encounter new methodological and professional challenges. The reconstruction of the past as legacy for the "new South Africa," as for new and critical geographies of the history of struggle, must eventually develop alternative directions and directives, contending with the "broken chains," covered tracks and interrupted narratives. It may be that Ruth First's life and work, after the fact, after the facts, suggest a model of their own kind for such inquiries.

Legalities

Such "points" for writing under cover as those that Mbeki had articulated, had been differently charted by the government in a series of legislative moves that were designed to consolidate the hegemony of a system of apartheid – dividing blacks from whites and denying, too, any attempts to rewrite the system or redraw the lines. Following on the pass laws dating back to the early days of the Union of South Africa, and in counterpoint to the revitalization of the ANC, the Defiance Campaign, the Freedom Charter, the bus boycotts and the mass protests in the 1950s, there were also on the part of the government those acts directed at the separation of the races: the Mixed Marriages Act 1949 and the Immorality Act 1957 illegalizing interracial sexual relations, the Group Areas Act which prohibited couples living together across the color line, the Reservation of Separate Amenities Act 1953, and the laws applying to Bantu Education. Each of these served to reinforce and secure the prosecution of a larger atlas of apartheid (see Bindman, *South Africa: Human Rights and the Rule of Law* (1988) and Christopher, *The Atlas of Apartheid* (1994)). More specifically still, a collocation of "security legislation" was elaborated in the 1950s and 1960s to prevent the retaking of space – public, cultural, social and political – from within which new forms of organization could be constituted. Primary among these were the Suppression of Communism Act 1950, which outlawed the Communist Party; the Unlawful Organizations Act 1960, according to which the ANC was eventually banned; the Sabotage Act 1962; and the Terrorism Act 1967. Additional laws buttressed these cordons, including the Criminal Law Amendment Act 1953, the Riotous Assemblies Act 1956, the Official Secrets Act 1956, the Defense Act 1957, the Explosives Act 1956, the Prohibition of Political Interference Act 1968, the Prevention of Dissemination of certain Doctrines against Bantu Law of the Bantu Administration Act 1959, the Publications and Entertainments Act 1963, the Customs and Excise Act 1964, the Prisons Act 1959, the Departure from the Union Regulations Act 1955, and the Defense of Property Law 1962. In addition, further legislation was enacted allowing for detention without trial, the most notorious of which was the 90 Day Detention Law, passed in 1963, and eventually extended to the 180 Day Detention Law in 1965 (see Cook, *South Africa: The Imprisoned Society* (1974)).

Prison Questions

> I'm not a revolutionary. I haven't the courage to risk prison. But I can't let them get away with it unwitnessed. I have to stay and oppose in my mind.
> Nadine Gordimer, *A Guest of Honour* (1983)

Ruth First was detained in 1963 – the first woman to be so halted – following the Rivonia arrests, according to the provisions of the 90 Day Detention Law and, when her term was renewed, she served a total of 117 days in detention. Her prison memoir of that period was accordingly entitled *117 Days*. Albie Sachs later acknowledged that precedence. Sachs, too, had been detained under the same law, for 168 days, and had thought to give that number as the title to his own "jail diary," but deferred to First's work (Sachs, 1990a). *117 Days*, originally published in

1965, tells of the compounded effects of the legislation on her own writing itinerary:

> Six hours before my first view of the cell, I had come out of the main reading-room of the University library. The project that week was how to choose atlases in stocking a library, and in my hand was a sheaf of newly scribbled notes:
>> pre-1961 atlases almost as obsolete for practical usage as a 1920 road map – evaluate frequency and thoroughness of revision, examine specialty maps, e.g. distribution of resources and population – look for detail plus legibility – check consistency of scale in maps of different areas – indexes – explanations of technical and cartographic terms, etc. etc. (*117 Days*, 1965, p. 17)

First's files concerning her recollections of the prison experience contain her full notes on the selection of atlases, suggesting the critical importance of these reference volumes to her work – whether in relocating South Africa on a new world historical map, or perhaps even in planning armed sabotage or providing escape routes for its operatives now under cover and on the run. First's student work in the university library, however, had come about as a result of her official banning as a journalist. As a result, as she tells it, discovering herself unable to find work with a newspaper, she had turned from "interviewing . . . probing . . . reporting" to "reference methods, cataloguing, and classification of books" (p. 17). The move, however, required a change of both place and pace: still another atlas, as it were, of the activism of an academic. *117 Days*, then, narrates her rediscovery – paradoxically, against the inquisitions of her interrogators and the silences of her cell – of her previous voluble career as a reporter and journalist/historian, from the writing on the walls of her cell, or the Bible she is allowed, to the "autobiography" she is asked to compose for her jailers, to the bits of paper that served to wrap sugar, or scraps of newspaper partially visible beyond her barred window, and finally the memoir itself.[1] Once an interviewer, she is now the interviewed, or rather the interrogated, with all the redistribution of locutory power that such disciplinary rearrangements entail. For already between the library and the cell, the police had taken First back to her home, where she was obliged to revisit her writing past and where they found a "single, forgotten copy of *Fighting Talk* [the South African Communist Party journal that First had edited], over-looked in the last clean-up in our house of banned publications." It would become all the more necessary, then, for First to restore that lapse in authorial responsibility and accountability: "I was going into isolation to face a police probe, knowing that even if I held out and they could pin no charge on me, I had convicted myself by carelessness in not clearing my house of illegal litera-ture: this thought became a dragging leaden guilt from then on" (p. 18). Following her release from prison, First went to England with her three daughters where she joined her husband, Joe Slovo, who had already fled South Africa shortly before her detention.

In England that same authorial self-query would become part of a second reconstruction of her prison experience for a BBC film in 1966. The issue of interrogation and the strategies for countering her questioners that had been paramount to her con-siderations at the time were no less so in the recapitulations of the encounters after the fact. In talking with Jack Gold, pro-ducer of the BBC program, and by way of mapping out the dynamics of the broadcast, First reiterates her concerns with the pressured coordinates of interrogation: "And I knew a helluva lot, really an awful lot," she says to Gold at one point. She goes on to indicate the ways in which such precautions had already again affected the narrative in the published book itself: "I took out of the book a paragraph in which I put what I knew because I thought it might give something away" (in Ruth First Papers).

"90 Days," "117 Days," "Interrogation South Africa" – the BBC production was variously named and eventually appeared on English television in March 1966 as "90 Days" – the final choice of a title making the production an interrogation of the law itself rather than a reprise of First's personal experience of detention. Important to its preparation, though, and as recorded by the transcript of her interview with producer Gold, were the establishment of the contestants to the plot and their positioning in the script. It was crucial, for example, that the arresting offi-cers of the Special Branch be identified in their full – if brute –

inadequacy, representing their own bureaucratic as well as political underdevelopment. Their ill-fitting clothes, their discomfort in an academic setting, their bumbling demeanor – all are mentioned as recognizable identifying markers of the men as agents of the security apparatus. Several further threads in the discussion contribute to the reconstruction of the prison narrrative for a popular viewing audience: the issue of interrogation – when, that is, to talk and when not to talk; and again the demands of this presentation to still another audience as another version of the dilemmas of telling. "90 Days" was to be broadcast to a metropolitan audience, this time not altogether familiar with the circumstances that had led to First's arrest. How much background on the situation in South Africa, for example, should be provided for British viewers? Should there be a narrator who would voice-over these details? What role would such a narrator play in the presentation of a docu-drama in which it is the very issue of "telling" that is at stake?

"I *must learn* to *think slowly*. I must tell them nothing" (emphasis in the original), First says recollectively in the pre-filming script. The considerations that oversaw such self-imposed restrictions are adumbrated in First's conversations with Jack Gold: "Suspense of waiting for interrogation really shakes you up," she says, and glosses again, "To keep the interrogation moving, so that you get something out of the next one and not give them too much – you think about every sentence you've said, has it given them any clue, tell them anything they didn't know before – *difficult for me*. Communicated in order to keep lines open yet not tell them something" (emphasis added). But if, in detention, the question of telling was of critical consequence, how to retell it now to a television viewing audience in England? Again, should there be a narrator? And what should that narrator report? At whose behest and to whose advantage? The very broadcast was itself an appeal, an address to another national public whose allegiances were otherwise also in question. Connections needed to be made, participation enlisted. How were the alliances to be established and drawn upon? As Jack Gold asks at the end of their interview: "I feel people will say 'well if she was a criminal what's so awful about trying to find out about things'. We have to suggest somehow that even if guilty of a crime, there are in an allegedly democratic society, there are legalities, there are the right ways of finding out. People will say 'what did she do?' and the moment you mention Rivonia and saboteur – 'what the hell did she expect?'" Expectations were indeed high and the South African government itself was quick to retort to the broadcast in a memo sent to the BBC:

> Where a programme (or a newspaper article, which has far less influence than a 55-minute television documentary) is based on a single source, that source should be unimpeachable. Could that be said of Miss Ruth First, writing about her detention by the South African police? All the advance publicity, the *Radio Times* and the programme itself described her as "the wife of a lawyer and the mother of three children." Would the viewer not have discounted quite a lot of Miss First's version of what happened to her had he [sic] been told by the BBC that she was an active Communist involved in a plot to overthrow the legal government of South Africa by violent means? Miss First has said publicly that is the position, but the BBC did not think it had any relevance for its viewers, and kept silent. (in Ruth First Papers)

Following her release from prison, Ruth First, like so many other banned persons from the period, had crossed the border and entered into exile. And so it happened too that her first book, about neighboring *South West Africa*, with its own beginnings in a dire confrontation with recalcitrant authorities in a library reading-room, was published in London. She would subsequently author, before her death by assassination in 1982, five more books: *Power in Africa* (originally entitled *The Barrel of a Gun: Political Power and the Coup d'Etat*, 1970), *The South African Connection: Western Investment in Apartheid* (1972, with Jonathan Steele and Christabel Gurney), *Libya: The Elusive Revolution* (1974), *Olive Schreiner* (1980, with Ann Scott) and *Black Gold: The Mozambican Miner, Proletarian and Peasant* (published posthumously in 1983). In addition to her editing of Mbeki's *The Peasants' Revolt*, she also assisted in the collection of Nelson Mandela's speeches and writings, *No Easy Walk to Freedom* (1990) and Oginga Odinga's Kenyan autobiography

Not Yet Uhuru (1967), which latter work occasioned her deportation at the time from Kenya. The very concept of authorship and its responsibilities and accountabilities were being given a new collaborative imperative as well as new collective parameters in First's writing.

Maps/Chronologies

> But you can't forgive and forget the past, if we don't know what the past was all about. Craig Williamson now, he's written open letters in the newspapers – No Craig! Come out, come out you bastard! Come and stand here and say you killed Ruth First! You did the Albie Sachs bomb and the bomb with Wal du Toit. The chap making those bombs is a personal friend of mine! So I said, we can forgive and forget, but then first we must know what it's all about.
>
> Dirk Coetzee in Bernstein, *The Rift* (1994)

If, as Grant Farred (1994) has argued (in the case of C. L. R. James), "[i]t is entirely appropriate that lives characterized by constant relocations and several ideological refashionings should resist definitive articulation in a single text," and furthermore that, "[i]n such deracinated existences, as if to echo their usually unpredictable geographical and uneven political movements, expression is more likely to be located in a number of texts" (p. 21), then the collection of books published by Ruth First over two decades and in the course of her exile following banning orders and detention in South Africa propose not only a critical map of a decolonizing Africa, a historical inquiry into the continent's development, but also an examination of the new directions and directives for the intellectual enjoined by those seismic changes. At work in each of these volumes, historically and site-specific though each is, and however implicitly, is an engaged tension between the politics of period and place on the one hand, and the critically conjunctural interventions undertaken by the writer-researcher on the other.

South West Africa (1963), for example, challenges South Africa's claims to that territory by examining not only the history

of that problematic trusteeship, but also contemporary international opinion, particularly as iterated in United Nations debates.
What would be the role of the UN in settling territorial disputes
and deciding political options? As First poses the question in the
introduction, "If the South West African issue expresses the essential dilemma of the apartheid state, it also touches the exposed
nerves of the UN" (p. 21). In turn, in *117 Days* (1965) the concern is not so much geopolitical regionalism and international
dominion, but that of the individual and the system, especially as
this system is presented through the policing apparatus of the
judicial and penal domains. *Political Power in Africa (The Barrel
of a Gun)* (1970), turns that question of the system into an investigation of the crises of change in newly independent, but already
neocolonial, African states and the regularization of the military
coup d'état as a means of transition. Does such a study require a
"'loose-leaf book, or wad of blank pages at the back'"?, as First
describes one colleague's reaction to the proposed study (p. 3). In
The South African Connection (1972), First's eventually decisive
reallocation of authorial rights through her published books, a
distribution that draws importantly on her experience as a journalist, is instantiated anew. Co-authored with Jonathan Steele
and Christabel Gurney, the book, anticipating the era of sanctions
and boycotts, insists on the conflict and/or collaboration between
narrow nationalisms and multinational capital: the "South
African connection" is precisely "western investment in
apartheid" – and the links between politics and business. With
Libya: The Elusive Revolution (1974), written on Muammar
Gadafi's assumption of power in that country, First breaches the
opportunistically "orientalist" distinction between "north
Africa" and "sub-Saharan Africa" and identifies a combined
regionalism and internationalism as the grounds of her ideological commitments and territorial purview. The map shifts again in
the biography of the early South African feminist, Olive Schreiner,
Olive Schreiner (1980), that First co-authored with Ann Scott.
First had been preparing a BBC radio broadcast on Schreiner in
1970 when she was asked to write the book. Several years later,
in 1974, she was interviewed by Ann Scott for *Spare Rib*, and
their collaboration, across disciplines and bridging ideological
dispositions and continental commitments, ensued. "The book,

still at the research stage, now turned into a collaboration as we became aware of the complementary perspectives each could bring to the subject – one that of a South African woman who had known of Olive Schreiner since childhood and been involved in radical underground politics in South Africa until the early Sixties; the other that of an English woman formed by feminism with its stress on a language of personal life" (p. 11). Finally and, as it would happen, posthumously, in *Black Gold* (1983), the issues of authorial claims and regional charters merge in generically radical ways. As First introduces the study of the "Mozambican miner, proletarian and peasant," "[t]his book has many authors" (p. ix). And as Alpheus Mangezi, himself a South African exile relocated in Maputo and one of those authors, recalls of the collective research work:

> I worked very closely with Ruth – her passion for the problems of the peasantry was so stimulating. Then after we had done the research on migrant labour and written the report, it was proposed that a book should be published. But more material was required, particularly interviews, so she gave me that responsibility. I drafted a scheme where I included work songs. This was something that I liked very much about Ruth: "Alpheus, I'm very doubtful about work songs." And I looked at her and said, "OK, I will do them all the same. So all right."
>
> I went and collected work songs. I was taken by car three hundred kilometers away from Maputo and left there. And I just walked around and talked with the people, and collected material. I couldn't carry it all – it was just incredible. So I returned. I took my tape recorder to Ruth and put on a cassette with one of the most moving songs that I had collected. I said, "You told me that you didn't believe in work songs. OK. Sit and listen." And she listened, and she was moved without understanding what it was all about. (Bernstein, 1994, pp. 28–9)

First's intellectual work remained in its own way consistent with the critical projects described by both Kanafani and Dalton. But the imperative, "to understand what the story meant from beginning to end," also raises that other demand of whether it is ever "enough to understand."

Narratives of a Banned Newspaper

"We Say Goodbye But We'll Be Back," was the headline of the final issue of *Spark*, datelined 28 March 1963. Like the *Guardian*, *Advance*, *Clarion*, and *New Age* before it, *Spark* was now banned in its turn by the South African government in its effort to put an end to the investigative reporting that over the decade had relentlessly exposed the abuses and contradictions which characterized the apartheid regime. On the front page of that final issue of *Spark*, its writers were featured prominently in photographs and their histories carried within: Govan Mbeki, Brian Bunting, Fred Carneson, M. P. Naicker – and Ruth First. A few months earlier, the paper had published a poem ominous in its very nostalgia and entitled "On Throwing Away a Bundle of Old Newspapers." The lyric commemorated the 27 December 1962 illegalization of the possession of any copies of the *Guardian*, *Advance* or *New Age* – the very ban which would eventually produce incriminating evidence against First on the occasion of her arrest. The poet (identified only as A. N.) wrote:

> Ah, what a world of suffering they revealed, these torn and
>   yellowed pages,
> The Bethals, Cato Manors, Windermeres, the lamentations of
>   the beloved country;
> But in this faithful record were not laments alone and weeping.
>   There were also
> The stirring epics of how we stood upright and threw back our
>   shoulders:
> How the miners came out in 46; how Dadoo and Naicker
>   fought the Ghetto Act;
> How the volunteers Defied; how again and again we Stayed at
>   Home
> In Egoli, Tekwini, Ebhai, in towns and villages, despite the sten
>   guns.
> And how we came from streets and factories and farms and
>   mines to Kliptown,
> And there beneath those sten guns made the Charter and the
>   Pledge.

And the dawn arrests when we Stood by Our Leaders. And the
   Long March from Alex.
Two thousand miles, day by day, to Victory. And Sharpeville.
   And Maritzburg.

First wrote for the *Guardian* from its inception, the beginnings of
a career in what Don Pinnock has called "a press with a mission."
Her writings for that newspaper not only accounted for the recur-
rence of daily events in South Africa, from the restrictions on
Cypriots (11 March 1948) to the bannings of a student production at the University of Witwatersrand of Shakespeare's *Othello*
(24 May 1957), but followed too such persistent issues as squat-
ters, boycotts, elections, trials, communism, trade unions and
labor. For the *Guardian* First contributed both signed and
unsigned articles and was variously identified as the paper's "parliamentary correspondent," "political correspondent," "industrial
correspondent," "Johannesburg correspondent" and "Cape Town
correspondent," tributes all to the geographies and geopolitics of
her probing inquiries. First continued with those written investigations through the many rebirthings of the papers following
their successively abortive bannings by the government. It was
important, as Pinnock points out, to "keep the red flag flying."
   The 1952 banning of the *Guardian*, the first newspaper to be
banned in South Africa for political reasons since 1824, had followed closely on the 1950 Suppression of Communism Act
which not only outlawed the Communist Party of South Africa
but identified by name its individual members – including First
and her husband Joe Slovo – as themselves among the ranks of
the banned. First's primary career in reporting and writing would
eventually earn her the credentials of detention, exile and death.
The single copy of *Fighting Talk*, a publication of the SACP
which First edited, found in her home by the Special Branch,
would remain as evidence of her written commitment, to be sure.
It displayed the contradictions of authorship, and – at least for
her interrogators at Marshall Square – of her threat to the state
itself. It would also endure in her own recollections of a mistaken
attachment to a certain construction of authorship itself. Indeed,
that same reporting would be cited by Wolfie Kodesh, a
colleague of Ruth First later at *New Age*, who remembered her

work and its consequential effects in the memoir that he wrote
for the journal *Sechaba* following her death: "But because of
the original story published by *New Age* through the pen of
Ruth First and photographs by Joe Gqabi and taken up later by
the national press, the ANC decided to launch the historic Potato
Boycott which is now written into the history of our movement.
It is sad to relate that both Cdes Ruth First and Joe Gqabi [who
was murdered in 1983] have perished at the hands of the racist
assassins and terrorists" (p. 32).

For all these papers Ruth First had written both attributed and
unattributed articles – in defiance not only of the South African
state restrictions but also of the conventions and norms of
authorship and authorial responsibility. Particular campaigns to
which her journalistic investigations importantly contributed
were revisited, however, in later articles that she published in
pamphlet and/or article form. "The Farm Labour Scandal,"
which appeared as a *New Age* pamphlet in July 1959, recovered
her provocative inquiries into the issue of forced labor on the
farms. Combining personal interview with the farm workers
with a studied review of the legislation that adjudicated the use
of pass laws as a sinister form of "recruitment" administered by
the Department of Native Affairs, First exposed the sway and the
connections between the territorial compartmentalizations of
apartheid and its systematic implementation of the premises of
capitalist expoitation. Similarly, the research that she carried out
from 1947 onwards into the specific abuses at the Bethal location
appeared in *Africa South* (1958), as did her narration of the bus
boycotts of 1955–6 (1957). Her ongoing work on migrant labor
more generally throughout southern Africa would be decisive in
her last, and posthumously published, book, *Black Gold* – the
most drastic wages of the fact and facts of writing having finally
been paid on receipt in Maputo of the desperate letter bomb
sent to her from across the border.

After the Facts

The long trail back home was barred by a ring of countries –
Rhodesia, friend of the apartheid regime; Namibia (South-West

Africa) completely under South African occupation; and the former British Protectorates, beholden to South Africa's economy
and cautious of antagonising their powerful neighbour.
Bernstein, *The Rift*, p. 145

Besides her prison memoir, *117 Days*, reconstructed from within
the very premises and strictures of the South African security
apparatus, only two of First's books deal directly with South
Africa itself – and even these two, *The South African Connection*
and *Olive Schreiner*, relate that country to an outside and more
explicitly to an international order of cultural politics and finance
capital, development narratives and biographical itineraries.
Whereas *The South African Connection* locates South Africa in
the collusive arenas of contemporary business and politics, cor-
porate investments and their colonial and postcolonial contexts,
dependency and national development, *Olive Schreiner* – the
only one of First's books that her youngest daughter, Robyn,
has read, "because that was different. Because that was about a
writer" (*The Rift*, p. 450) – relates the biographical story of a
white South African woman at the turn of the nineteenth and
twentieth centuries. Schreiner had lived part of her adult life in
England and would eventually achieve international renown for
her novel, *The Story of an African Farm*, set in South Africa and
first published in England in 1883, as well as her study of
"woman and labour" (1911); no less redoubted was her association in England with the life and work of Havelock Ellis. First's
and Scott's co-authored book on Schreiner perhaps then assumes
an autobiographical significance in Ruth First's own bibliography, an attempt to recover an earlier history, the purviews of an
antecedent generation, of many of the same issues that First herself would, towards the other end of the century, confront: from
the peasantry and modes of production to the complex relations
between periphery and metropolis, particularly as these are delineated in the course of a personal life history. In the radio play,
"Olive Schreiner: A Portrait," that she wrote for the BBC (these
radio plays also included the stories of Pancho Villa and the
Dolfuss Assassination [in the Ruth First Papers]) and which was
broadcast in December 1970, a narrator introduces the subject:
"At the turn of the century, a South African woman was uttering

grave predictions about her country" (ms., p. 1). Those same predictions would be reiterated by the fact of the play at the end of
the century, but First was no less interested in Schreiner's writing
objectives – the exigencies of combining a "creative imagina-
tion" with a relentless "contact with any facts" (ms., p. 3) and
resisting the exoticisations and political apologias available from
Piccadilly or the Strand. Schreiner's years of exile in England
had been characterized by the passionate struggle to work, and
the difficulties of poor health and social distractions: "Why,"
Schreiner wrote – and as she was no less prophetically cited by
First – "must I always write in blood?" (ms., p. 20). But
Schreiner, unlike Ruth First, was to return to South Africa, where
she would challenge British designs on the country and notori-
ously attack Cecil John Rhodes as not a statesman at all, but
rather a "financier without scruples" (ms., p. 30). As First would
later tell Ann Scott, Olive Schreiner "needs to be rescued as a
political thinker, and a political person. And she's only just coming into her own in South Africa. But perhaps she excites me
more as a liberated, if struggling woman. She felt about her life
that it was not being dogged by illness that she minded, it was
not being able to work" (*Spare Rib*, 1974). Ruth First worked
with Ann Scott in the important collaboration that resulted in the
co-authored biography *Olive Schreiner*. And as Scott would in
her turn tell Susan Gardner (*Hecate*, ms., 1980), that collaboration was itself a critical reading of differences in feminisms,
cultures and generations – further overdetermined by First's own
experience of exile in England and her involvement in remaking
South African history.

In April 1994, with the first democratic elections in South
Africa and the election of Nelson Mandela as South Africa's first
black president, those issues discovered still new, radically altered
possibilities on a remapped political terrain. Personal lives were
no less dramatically transformed as individuals left the underground movement for places in the bureaucratic echelons,
parliamentary positions, ministerial posts and cabinet. That same
year saw the publication of two (among myriad others that
accompanied this change) works that sought to classify – ground
even – what had now become a passing, if not altogether past,
order. While A. J. Christopher's *Atlas of Apartheid* provides a

cartography – from townships, homelands and city-planning to domestic interiors and regional stratagems – of the history of apartheid South Africa, Hilda Bernstein's *The Rift* chronicles the personal narratives of South Africans in exile throughout the world: in ANC training camps and schools in Zambia and Tanzania, in the anti-apartheid movement in England, the United States and in European capitals, and before the assemblies of such organizations as the United Nations, the Non-Aligned Movement, or the Organization of African Unity. Two political geographies, if not three, are contrived and contested in these accounts: the national, the regional, and the international – geographies that Ruth First's own books, published in the two decades between her exile in 1963 and her death in 1982, had earlier sought historically to critique.

Was it water for the living or mass graves for the dead that were to be the first order of priority asked newscasters, aid workers and policy-makers in July 1994, as hundreds of thousands of refugees from neighboring Rwanda faced death across the border in Zaire where they had fled following the latest four months of strife in their country? The question of United Nations intervention that had been raised by First in *South West Africa* three decades previously had been revised by this time; the political had since been divided between the military and the humanitarian – not just in central Africa, but also in Somalia, Haiti, northern Iraq and Bosnia – and for all the division there seemed little difference to be made. South Africa declined to send troops of its own to Rwanda, maintaining that in its first days of a new national order it could little afford to manage continental catastrophes. But South Africa's complicated dispositions toward Rwanda within the new geographies of struggle were no less critical to the country's future than they had been in the course of its past. And in November 1995 President Mandela would publicly argue for sanctions against Nigeria following the executions of environmental and human rights activist Ken Saro-Wiwa and his eight comrades. Indeed, as First's *South West Africa*, *The South African Connection*, and *Black Gold* argued at the beginnings of three respective decades, South Africa's place within global politics is decidedly indicative of the changing parameters of global order.

In the introduction to *South West Africa* in 1963, First had written that "South West Africa is a test case of UN efficiency. Principles have been proclaimed, but action persistently deferred. The resolutions have been strong enough, but Dr Verwoerd, a past master in the use of words, is not afraid of them. South Africa has used evasion, procrastination, boycotts, and sulks; now open defiance, now niggardly negotiation; but after six-teen years her stubborn refusal to budge before the near-unanimous United Nations decisions presents a challenge to the whole authority of the world organization" (p. 19). Three years later, in 1966, the International Court at The Hague had returned a negative decision to the petition presented by Ethiopia and Liberia on behalf of South West Africa, determining that the petitioners had no legal standing before the court on this partic-ular issue. Ruth First would be obliged to write again, in "South-West Africa" (1966), that "[i]n what has sarcastically been called a 'non-judgement' the International Court at The Hague on July 18 rejected the case of Liberia and Ethiopia (act-ing for the African States) against South Africa in which they charged that the application of apartheid to South-West Africa violates the 'sacred trust' of the mandate" (p. 419). That "trust" was part of the legacy of the League of Nations and the mandate system it had established to deal with the residues of colonial policy and administration following the First World War. As Eduardo Mondlane, president of the Mozambique Liberation Front (Frelimo), argued at a conference convened by Ronald Segal and Ruth First to discuss the case of South West Africa as a "travesty of trust," what was at international issue were pre-cisely national self-determination and independence. From the League of Nations and its mandate system (Article 22 of the Covenant of the League of Nations) – a "system for the dis-posal of the spoils of the common enemy" (p. 268) – to the United Nations and its trusteeship system (Chapters XII and XIII of the Charter of the United Nations Organization), the disposal of those same spoils had yet to be decided. Neither self-government nor independence had been acknowledged and the case of South West Africa would remain outstanding until 1989–90, when elections would be held to determine the self-government of the new state of Namibia. In the meantime, however, the contemporary questions of "humanitarian intervention," United Nations peacekeeping/peacemaking forces, economic sanctions, political embargoes and boycotts were rediscovering new ideological parameters and geographic limits in a "post bi-polar" world order.

Whereas in 1963 South Africa had categorically refused the jurisdiction of the international community over its trusteeship in South West Africa, asserting instead its own sovereign claims to the territory, not ten years later, the "drive to win friends and influence in the EEC took Mr Vorster to Paris on his first visit to Europe" (*The South African Connection*, p. 36). *Black Gold*, by contrast to *South West Africa*'s internationalism, insists on the significance of the more local transformations to the regional production and culture of both landscape and political projections in such work songs as that cited by Mangezi: "I would like to join my husband – he left for the mines; but there is no way of getting there. The Nkomati is in flood. I would like to go back to my people. I come from across the Limpopo River, but lobola has been paid; and since he has not said he is divorcing me, I cannot go back to my people. The Limpopo is in flood, I'm stuck here" (*The Rift*, p. 29). On the other hand, according to Rob Nixon's commentary on contemporary South Africa, "[n]o other post-World War II struggle for decolonization has been so fully globalized; no other has magnetized so many people across such national divides, or imbued them with such a resilient sense of common cause." Nixon goes on to point out the very paradoxes of how an "ideology dedicated to the sundering of communities set in motion vast transnational processes of incorporation – the divestment campaign, and the boycotts of culture, sport, trade, oil, and military hardware" (1994, p. 1).

First, meanwhile, even as she envisioned these eventualities, wrote of the cordons created by South Africa at the same time that it sought to establish inroads with metropolitan corridors of power and entry into the backrooms of multinational capital. In a series of articles written between 1972 and 1978 for various Italian editors (in Ruth First Papers), she elaborated on the complicated histories written across the territories of the sub-continent. In "The Oppenheimers: Father and Son" ("I Protagonisti dell'Africa" 1972), for example, First continues the

critical narrative initiated by Olive Schreiner's challenge to Cecil
Rhodes at the beginning of the century. Opening her historical
account with the arrival of the Dutch in southern Africa in 1652,
and following it through the discovery of gold and diamonds in
the nineteenth century, the Boer War and the later twentieth century contest between the dictates of apartheid and the needs of an
expanding industrial economy, First revises a family saga as crucial to a national, political economy, narrative. It was a history
that she continued in "Class Structure and Struggle in South
Africa," written "for" Joe Slovo from his article in *Southern
Africa: The New Politics of Revolution*, because, as she informed
the editors of *Politica Internazionale*, her husband was at the
time "working in Luanda and [because] he left before he could
send you the article, he left the task to me" (8 October 1976). At
issue in this essay are the combined pressures of race and class
and their particular manifestations in the South African context,
and as analysed by the Freedom Charter and articulated in the
SACP's Programme with its readings of a "colonialism of a special type." Not just the history of the region, but its
historiography is crucial to First's writing. In "Colonial Regimes
in Southern Africa," then, which was eventually published in
Dizionario critico de storia contemporanea, a volume which also
included articles by Walter Rodney on precolonial Africa, by
Giovanni Arrighi on neocolonialism in Africa, and by Terence
Ranger on African resistance to colonialism, First insists on the
interactions of the national, the regional and the international –
for the immediacies of the struggle no less than for the retro-
spectives of the historian.

> Since the liberation of Angola and Mozambique, colonial regimes
> in Southern Africa have been reduced to three countries. Each of
> the three has distinctive conditions. Namibia [South West Africa]
> is virtually a colony of South Africa, with her economy limited to
> primary extraction in the interests of South African and interna-
> tional capital. Rhodesia's ruling class is constituted by a white
> power bloc reminiscent of the forces in control of the South
> African state at a much earlier stage of development. But
> although, in an analysis of the three societies, their historic peri-
> odisation is different, and structural conditions have dictated

different processes of economic growth, and a different constel-
lation of ruling class forces, the three territories need to be
analysed together for their systemic similarity. (ms., pp. 1–2)

Furthermore, First goes on, insisting again on the combined politics of independence and an economics of dependence, a "grave
limitation of almost all history-writing of the sub-continent is
that, though common methodological approaches prevail, its
various territories have been treated as distinctive, each with its
own body of evidence and interpretation" (ms., p. 2).

Like Basil Davidson, whose recent *The Black Man's Burden:
Africa and the Curse of the Nation State* (1992) draws urgent
comparisons – and contrasts – between Africa on the one hand,
and a consolidating Japan and a disintegrating Eastern Europe
on the other, First's book-length studies importantly raise the
question of "Where in the world is Africa?" – or, more specifically, "Where in the world is South Africa?"[2] Davidson's
analysis, which argues on behalf of a "native African model of
community self-government" (p. 51), has been critiqued as a
"continuation of the original anti-colonial standpoint, of which
it is the most distinguished surviving exponent, at least in
English" (Leys, 1994, p. 37), but its insistence on regionalist
approaches as against nativist, reductively nationalist, or even
essentialist models, proposes not just atavistic survivals but a
renewal and reactivation of an internationalism that had once
animated the national liberation struggles of the decades of anti-
colonialism and decolonization.

Much as Nelson Mandela had refused, on Ted Koppel's ABC
broadcast of the *Nightline* town meeting in June 1990 following
his release from prison a few months earlier, to disassociate himself from Cuba, Libya or the PLO, or, a month later, in visiting
the Republic of Ireland, to disavow a solidarity with the Irish
republican armed struggle, South Africa was, in its post-election
period, renegotiating its position in international politics: rein-
statement in the United Nations, membership in such other
world political bodies as the International Labor Organization
and the Organization of African Unity, economic ties with the
European Union, Japan and the United States, the World Bank
and the International Monetary Fund. At the same time,

however, it also asserted its adherence to the "Group of 77" developing countries. "South Africa," said Foreign Minister Alfred Nzo, "understands the dichotomy between the developed and developing worlds since apartheid created a similar social and economic disparity" (Reuters, 24 June 1994). The lines drawn, the encomiums of traditonal development narratives, parameters and perimeters questioned by Ruth First in such works as *South West Africa, The South African Connection*, as too in *Black Gold*, are being submitted again now to other building blocs, new designs, alternative plans, with significant consequences for redesignating "spheres of influence" no less than "new geographies of struggle". Could Ruth First, in other words, have returned to her old ways in a new South African history? Others – writers and political activists – would experiment with the various routes of recall.

Reporting Back

With "transparency" as an explicit hallmark of its political priorities and policy imperatives, the new South African government, under the presidency of Nelson Mandela, elected in the country's first ever democratic elections in April 1994, assumed its offices the following month. Transparency meant that the government's actions, decision-making processes and programmatic implementations would be open – available, visible, accessible – to the public scrutiny. While the workings of such a practice of transparency – and crucial as this might be to democratic rule – are difficult even in the present circumstances, their application to an examination of apartheid, South Africa's past, are yet still more problematic. Not only was the establishment of a Truth Commission – like those in Argentina and Brazil following the years of dictatorship, or that mandated by the peace agreement in El Salvador – still debated, but the question also remained as to what would be the consequences of such a commission's findings. What kind of accountability, for example, should be assigned to those named by an inquiry? What recourse and redress will the victims have? To whom, indeed, should the information be made available? Nor was the issue of a general amnesty, like that unilaterally declared in March 1993 by El Salvador's then president Cristiani, resolved.

While the history – both infamous and legendary – of South African apartheid and the struggle against its abuses has become part of the debates even within South African historiography, occasioned by the release of memoirs, reports, affidavits, newly revealed Special Branch files and archives such as the Robben Island materials housed in the Mayibuye Centre at the University of the Western Cape, new narratives and new stories are contributing now to still another record enabled by the very possibility of return – not just to the past, but to South Africa itself. AnnMarie Wolpe's (1994) *The Long Way Home*, Ronnie Kasrils' (1993) *Armed and Dangerous*, and the many interviews collected by Hilda Bernstein in *The Rift*, are each structured around the question of return and its inevitable effect for reconstructing both prospectively and retrospectively the new South Africa. Each of the authors had played significant if differing roles in the historic organized resistance to apartheid and the alternative beginnings to their narratives are thus critical to its recounting. Bernstein, whose husband "Rusty" was acquitted in the 1963 Rivonia trial, had been active in the Congress Alliance in the 1950s and left South Africa illegally in 1964 for exile in England and continued writing and public speaking. Following her husband's escape from prison in 1963, Wolpe, who had herself been briefly detained, fled that same year, also to London. She was eventually joined by Harold and their three children and became prominent in education and women's studies in England. Kasrils also fled in 1963 but, as the subtitle to his memoir, "my underground struggle against apartheid," indicates, his exile was spent in furthering the work of the armed resistance, largely in the several African countries in which the ANC had established its training camps. The year 1963, then, and the security forces' raid on the Rivonia farmhouse which had provided a central venue for the struggle's organizing and activism inside South Africa is just as crucial to all three histories as it is to the larger resistance account.

If 1961 and the formation of Umkhonto we Sizwe had marked a radical new departure for the struggle from non-violent means of opposition to armed struggle, the Rivonia detentions are

generally acknowledged to have arrested that development itself
and to have decimated the movement's leadership, sending its
most prominent figures into exile – or to life imprisonment. But
given that common crisis, Kasrils, Wolpe and Bernstein each
begin – and continue – their stories differently. For Kasrils, the
story opens in 1989, with his clandestine and preliminary return
to South Africa. Mandela was still in prison and, writes Kasrils,
"Although the possibility of negotiating with the Pretoria government was arising, expectations of progress were generally
uncertain and the ANC remained banned" (p. 3). It is with the
announcement, communicated to her by a fellow exile at
Middlesex Polytechnic, of the unbanning of the ANC and the
SACP that AnnMarie Wolpe introduces the recounting of her
own personal "long way home." By contrast, Hilda Bernstein
describes her complementary project of narrating through oral
history the South African experience of exile as one which she
started "at a time when many South Africans had left their
homes as long as thirty years ago, and there was still no hope of
return" (p. xii). According to Bernstein, "Exiles are those who
leave with the intention of returning." And, as she goes on,
"Sometimes refugees become exiles. And some exiles, losing the
intention of returning and abandoning political involvement,
become emigrés. But even these often remain involved with the
passion of apartheid politics, however peripherally" (p. xii). That
very passion, in nonetheless markedly different ways, distin-
guishes these three volumes, all published in the same year as the
elected beginning of the new South Africa.

If *The Long Way Home* opens with the announcement of
unbanning orders, that announcement is quickly followed by
Wolpe's own conflicted response that alternates between the realization that she "can go home again" and the question of where,
after all, after twenty-seven years in London exile, is home. Her
husband, Harold Wolpe, had remained all that time an activist in
the anti-apartheid movement. Employed in the Sociology
Department of Essex University though, he is "disenchanted with
the department, which fails to give him any tangible recognition
for things he has written which have had a major impact in
South Africa and among Africanists in general" (p. 10).
AnnMarie, too, had maintained – or rather re-established – her

links with the movement. "The ANC is now my organisation – I joined it only a few years ago," she writes, commenting further that "I have moved away from what I had felt was an almost moribund feminist movement in the UK, and found a new home in the ANC" (p. 8). It is precisely her work in London, however, which leads her to question the viability of her own return now: "A Women's Studies course such as I have been running at the Poly is not really transferable to South Africa. My brand of feminism is really Eurocentric. Questions relating to the construction of gender identity somehow do not seem entirely appropriate in a country where the ravages of apartheid have overridden any gender issues" (p. 16). Between "Going Home: February 1990–June 1991" and the narrative's "Epilogue: July 1993," Wolpe tells the much longer story of "The Escape: June–August 1963," the taut events that had led her out of South Africa in the first place, combining both her husband's story of arrest, detention and escape, and her own participation in the effort at his release. But even with the conclusion to the book, the story has not ended. Working at the Centre for Adult and Continuing Education at UWC, Wolpe's "brand of feminism" has not been called upon, no demands made, and she reflects still that "There is a sense – and Harold shares this view with me – of a resistance to utilise to the full the abilities and capacities of returning exiles – except, of course, for those who fitted full-time into ANC structures" (p. 277).

Ronnie Kasrils tells a very different story. Described by the South African police as "armed and dangerous," the title of his memoir, he was pursued by the security forces even on his return in 1990. A leading member of the South African Communist Party and former head of military intelligence in the ranks of Umkhonto we Sizwe, his narrative focuses on that work during his years of exile. Framed like Wolpe's by the present tenses – and tensions – of return, Kasrils' retrospective is otherwise engaged with the difficulties of fighting one's way home. The struggle in the military training camps which he relates has itself become part of the current debate on "transparency." In 1993, for example, following questions from Amnesty International, the ANC – unlike the South African government – admitted to the imperative of a critical investigation into its own practices in treating disaffection and defection in its ranks, practices that Kasrils reviews in his personal narrative. That narrative also presents a political history of the SACP and its internal discussions concerning the place of dissent in its development. There was, for example, the "tension between security and personal choice, which mirrored the contradiction in countries attempting to build socialism" (p. 177). Kasrils' story also ends in anticipation: "Those who hold the reins of power, regardless of their slogans and their political colours, must understand that unless they serve the interests of the people, they will never succeed" (p. 368).

Many of the exiles interviewed by Hilda Bernstein trained in those same camps in which Kasrils worked. Indeed, like Peta and Tessa Wolpe, AnnMarie's daughters, Kasrils himself and his wife Eleanor are among *The Rift*'s interviewees. He spoke with Bernstein in Harare in 1990, Eleanor in London that same year. *The Rift*, which includes the stories from more than one hundred such encounters, is organized chronologically, according to the period in which the interlocutors went into exile, and geographically, according to their place of exile. As Bernstein wrote, "Each wave brought out its own type of people" (p. xvi). Such differences as there were among them in the circumstances of departure must necessarily also affect the conditions of their return. The interviews take place throughout southern Africa (except in South Africa itself), in England, in other European countries, in the United States and in Canada. They tell of women who left children behind, as well as women who gave birth in exile, of young men who continued their studies abroad, of children (like Shawn, Gillian and Robyn Slovo)[3] who resisted the political commitments of their parents in order to find lives of their own in countries not their own, of fighting, of poetry and public speaking, and assassination attempts on the exiles – and the constant struggle, emotional, political, and armed – over the penultimate question of return.

In each of these works, however, return is only the beginning, a beginning with a past, to be sure, but which anticipates another future. The interviews collected over the years in *The Rift*, like *The Long Way Home* and *Armed and Dangerous*, go far in making the issues – demands both immediate and visionary, questions of feminism, of human rights, of new and popular histories – of reconstructing a new South Africa viable and visible. They commit their own kind of truth and also reveal the difficulty of the transition from a culture in which secrecy and the choice between "to talk or not to talk" was a matter of life and death, for oneself and for others, to a social order in which "transparency" is the hallmark of new possibilities. One of those possibilities is the writing of these books; another is that of reading them in South Africa.

From Rivonia to Soweto: Atlases and Genealogies

The critical atlas – national, regional, international, from South West Africa to Libya, in prison, in the library, at universities, and in exile, in interviews and in interrogation – elaborated over the preceding decades in First's books, articulates as well with the specifically critical historical conjuncture reviewed in these narratives of return: that of national liberation movements, resistance struggles, decolonization and the transition to independence of formerly colonized countries across the globe. When First died in 1982, that conjunctural moment had been largely consummated, but her work, it might be argued, and spanning even as it does the two decisive "generations" of the contemporary South African narrative, remains informed by the political imperatives of historical crisis. Like Hilda Bernstein, for example, many readers of the South African story of the last half of the century identify two decisive dates: the massacre at Sharpeville in 1960 when security forces opened fire on a crowd of silent protestors of the infamous pass laws, killing more than sixty people and wounding scores of others, that led eventually to the formation of Umkhonto we Sizwe and the initiation of the armed struggle; and the Soweto rebellion in 1976, when schoolchildren, demanding the right to study in English rather than Afrikaans, seen as the language of their oppressors, led the way into a new era of protest and struggle. *The Rift* had further identified the generational constructions of departure determined significantly by the unfolding of events within the country. In the 1950s and early 1960s, for example, those who left were "mainly adult, often middle-aged, and highly political, with a history of engaging in public political struggle." The 1976 Soweto rebels, by contrast, "came out with no history in their heads." And then, in the 1980s, the exiles "came from the reborn internal resistance to the terror, a wave of determined people, black and white, hardened by life-threatening activity in the popular armed and unarmed resistance, experienced in work both above and underground" (pp. xvi–xvii).

The historical and theoretical significance of the Soweto uprising was, two years afterwards in 1978, the subject of a critical debate between Archie Mafeje and Ruth First in the pages of the *Review of African Political Economy*. For Mafeje, Soweto was a "historical event of great significance. It threw into relief a number of issues which had preoccupied many South African cadres in exile" (p. 25). Among those issues, as First pointed out in her response, Mafeje identified the relationship between students and workers and the national struggle, the relationship between internal and external forces and their very different forms of organization, the relationship of the armed struggle to the political struggle and finally the connection between the national revolution and the socialist revolution (p. 93). Mafeje emphasized a historical perspective, one that not only identified the significance of the placement and positioning of Soweto 1976 in that chronology, but also examined the ideological as well as geopolitical disposition of the South African movements now in exile. Thus, if Soweto was a "historical event of great significance," Mafeje went on to maintain that "[w]hatever the failures and subsequent disillusionment, it must not be forgotten that the older movements have a history and are an important part of the South African political heritage." And furthermore, Mafeje adds, "the differences between them should not be brushed aside, for they are real and ideologically determined" (p. 26). Among those differences – with which First will take critical issue – are the class identification of migrant workers, the respective forms of organization, and the status of the leadership within the movements themselves. First, however, challenges Mafeje that the "assertion of only maximalist perspectives at the cost of tactics for immediate struggle produces an outlook that is adventurist and quietist at the same time" (p. 97). Acknowledging with

Mafeje the critical juncture represented by the Soweto uprising, First nonetheless elaborates a different historical narrative: "Soweto, although it reached unprecedented heights, is in the tradition of mass struggles in South Africa which began by asserting often fairly minimalist demands – and precipitately found themselves in full-scale confrontation with the power of the state." In that tradition she identifies the 1946 miners' strike (which she had reported as a journalist) and the Defiance Campaign of the 1950s (in whose organization she had participated) (p. 96). For First, then, the larger problem still remains that of "*how to assess mass struggles this side of the revolution*" (emphasis in the original, p. 96).

"This side of the revolution" was precisely where Ruth First had lived, had struggled, had written – and it was there too where she eventually died. "This side of the revolution" – a geography, a history and a political commitment.

After the Fact: Reconstructions of an Individual

In the Death Squads there's apartheid of sorts. I was handling the blacks in Botswana/Lesotho/Swaziland and South Africa, Williamson only handled whites. Him and Johan Coetzee had their little special reasons, why this one and why that? Agh, it's just so senseless. I don't think there's any sense, there's any logic in it. Why choose Ruth First? She was at the University of Maputo, why kill her?
Dirk Coetzee in *The Rift*, p. 213

The morning of her death, I woke early. Not from her typing but from the lack of it . . .

A group of mourners waited beside the coffin. It was closed – on my father's request.

I was grateful that I did not have to see her in front of those embarrassed, uncomfortable men. And yet it would have helped to see what she looked like after she died.

When I think of it, I see what my father saw after they called him in – her legs, and untouched at their end, a pair of elegant, undamaged high-heeled shoes that were her passion. He, who had witnessed death by violence before, didn't go further. I would not have either. And yet, perhaps, if I had seen her, some part of my horror at what the explosion must have done to her might have been laid to rest.

Gillian Slovo, "A mother remembered and mourned," *Weekly Mail and Guardian* (20–26 January 1995)

Slovo still points out that the Eastern bloc was not all "tyranny and evil and murder and mayhem":

You're talking about a world that pioneered the modern eight-hour day, women's equality and free education. Every segment of the welfare capitalist world originated in the socialist world and the battle between the two had an impact on the more tolerable conditions in the capitalist world.

He admitted that his own doubts began in the mid-1960s but he chose to remain silent because he had seen the alternative close at hand. His wife, fiercely independent, was, he said, side-lined by the movement. He said he had differences with her on the issue.

The choice that you face is whether you can continue to contribute to the struggle or not. At that stage, independence was just not tolerated. It was part of the sickness we tried to get away from eventually.

For me, the question was: do I now take a lecturer's job in London? In retrospect I would have made a big mistake if I'd allowed my doubts, which were growing and growing, to lead to a withdrawal.

Joe Slovo, Interview with Philip van Niekerk, *Weekly Mail and Guardian* (9–14 December 1994)

A banner headline on the front page of South Africa's *Weekly Mail and Guardian*, in the 29 July–4 August 1994 issue just short of the "first one hundred days" of the new South African government, read "Maharaj reveals stolen NIS files." Mac Maharaj, former underground leader in the ANC and a cabinet minister in the new government, had released a set of uncovered files documenting his work in "operation Daisy" from 1977 to 1980 and kept by the South African National Intelligence Service (NIS). The release of the files (which are now housed at the

Mayibuye Center of the University of the Western Cape) sig-
nalled a dramatic move in the contest over the past being waged
by the new government's efforts to engage a Truth Commission
inquiry into the decades of apartheid rule and anti-apartheid
struggle. Such documents and files, the archives of investigation
past and present, were crucial, it was argued by many, to such an
inquiry. Accompanying the headline were photographs of
Maharaj, to be sure, but also of Craig Williamson who had done
the spying that provided the research for the files, and of law
professor John Dugard, journalist Patrick Laurence and "exiled
activist" Ruth First – each named for various reasons in the
pages of the files. The continuation of the story on page two
identified Ruth First as one of the assassination targets of
Williamson's operations. A week later, however, in the following
issue (5–11 August 1994), a letter to the editor from Joaquim
Martins Cardosa (of Bedfordview, Johannesburg) questioned the
report, arguing instead that "First was accidentally killed by a
letter-bomb addressed to Professor Aquino de Braganca, the late
director of the Centre for African Studies at the Eduardo
Mondlane University in Maputo," and going on to conclude
that "At the time of the attempt on Professor Braganca's life, he
was one of President [Samora] Machel's closest advisers. In 1982,
the president's Frelimo government was shifting its posture
towards the Western bloc. Machel and Braganca died in a plane
crash in October 1986" (p. 28). More than just evidence of a
rivalry in a sweepstake for a place in the assassination hall of
fame, this letter identifies rather the political stakes in such legacies. While the letter writer's representation of Machel's own
political directions can well be disputed in finer detail (Machel
died in a plane crash in 1986 during the negotiations of the
Nkomati Accords between South Africa and Mozambique), the
implication is more significantly that assassination takes place for
precisely political reasons, a recognition that corpuses as much as
corpses were at issue, and have yet to be laid to rest.

Indeed, the Maharaj files maintained by the NIS from 1977
to 1980 address this very concern. Distressed at the new inroads
of the ANC/CP (the files make excessively clear the connection – if not identification – that the security agency wanted to
establish between the ANC and the SACP) in organizational

activity both in and outside South Africa, the very first page
identifies the direction of such inroads: "(i) The ANC/CP was
attempting to gain dominance over all its opposition, both inter-
nally and externally; (ii) That the ANC/CP was making an
all-out effort to build up networks inside the Republic of South
Africa (RSA) (with an external infrastructure to support these
networks.); (iii) As a direct result of the above, the centre of
gravity of the ANC/CP was shifting from London to Africa,
with Lusaka as headquarters" (NIS files, ms.). Maharaj's files,
which were disclosed by their subject on this (now the other)
side of the revolution, mention Ruth First twice: once as coor-
dinator of the Maputo office of the Internal Reconstruction and
Development Department (IRDD) allegedly (according to the
files) overseen by Maharaj, and then as a close contact of the
Cachalia family (the NIS was particularly worried here about
the influence of the ANC/CP on Indian politics in South Africa).
And yet, a short half year after the files' release, and following
the death from cancer of Joe Slovo, husband of Ruth First and
Housing Minister in the new government who had been head of
the SACP, an executive committee member of the ANC, and
leader in Umkhonto we Sizwe, in a story accompanying the
memorials and *testimonios* to his leadership and the coverage of
his mass-attended funeral, a curious version of an obituary
appeared. The banner headlines in another of South Africa's
weekly newspapers, *New Nation*, announced: "Slovo's Wife's
Killer on Indemnity List" (20–26 January 1995). According to
the story inside, Craig Williamson's name appeared on the "list
of 3500 people granted indemnity for crimes committed during
the apartheid era."

When Joyce Moodley, in prison in August 1964, had been
shown the writer's picture, she recognized Ruth First, but the
cognizance was not to the satisfaction of the detainee's interlocutors: "What did she do? I don't know . . . she was a
journalist, she was taking photographs and she was writing"
(*The Rift*, pp. 33–4). Who? what? was the "real thing"? The revolutionary and party cadre who had a fondness for Italian shoes,
as so many of her acquaintances and intimates still recall? Or, as
others remember, sometimes with lingering caution, a woman
with a "sharp tongue," a woman who "did not suffer fools

easily" (see Kasrils, 1993, and Podbrey, 1993, for example). Nearly three decades after Joyce Moodley's interrogation, in the introduction to the Ruth First Memorial Lecture that she presented in 1991, Victoria Brittain remembered two more, different again, portraits, recollected images that suggest why Ruth First might have been so critical not only to the reconnaissances of the Special Branch and the South African security forces, but to a contemporary analysis and recognition of southern African politics in the post-Cold War (or post bi-polar world) order:

> The first picture – it must have been in January of 1981 in London – is of her extreme and unveiled impatience with one of those interminable ANC meetings in which a platform full of men in suits read long, dull speeches with no concrete facts and many pious hopes about the situation in South Africa.
>
> The second, during the same visit to London, is the fastidious precision with which she rewrote chunks of an article about her research at Eduardo Mondlane University. Ruth had agreed to put her name to the article in the *Guardian* provided I did the draft from a long conversation we had. Her open scepticism that I could possibly get such an article published in a mainstream newspaper rather wounded me and I was determined to prove her wrong. (p. 22)

As Albie Sachs too recalls of his former comrade, in the introduction to the re-edition of her prison memoirs, First was "white in an overwhelmingly black movement" (p. 8), an "intellectual of middle-class background in a struggle dedicated to the emancipation of the workers" (p. 9), a "woman in a male-dominated world" (p. 10), and a "critic in a movement that required a high degree of discipline" (p. 11).

But in acknowledging that same exemplary status of intellectuals, Stuart Hall reminds their readers of another precaution: "major intellectual and political figures are not honored simply by celebration. Honor is accorded by taking his or her ideas seriously and debating them, extending them, quarreling with them, and making them live again" (cited in Farred, 1994, p. 23). So too her compatriot and collaborator, Ronald Segal, would note at a London memorial commemorating Ruth First's death: "Her life was a political act. Equally her death was another kind of political act. So too memorials to her must be political acts."

Reporter, librarian, political detainee, partisan, professor, theoretician and historian, researcher – Ruth First's legacy – her corpus like her corpse – continues testifying, now to the Truth Commission as before to the Special Branch, and reinstantiating a politics of dissent, another sense of mission: "after the fact" and "after the facts."

PART III

NEW GEOGRAPHIES
OF STRUGGLE

Everyone is entitled to a social and international order in which the rights and freedoms set forth in the Declaration can be fully realized.
Article 28: Universal Declaration of Human Rights (1948)

Ghassan Kanafani died in 1972, Roque Dalton in 1975 and Ruth First in 1982. While their lifelong work had been committed to the international struggle against imperialism and on behalf of national liberation and decolonization, the decade of their deaths witnessed the closing phases of an epochal transformation, from colonialism to an age called "postcolonial." Their writing – itself a critical interrogatory into the global distortions of an unequal distribution of rights and resources – was call enough, however, for their own interrogations at the hands of those who had authorized such distortions. It was often an occasion, too, for political debate within their own political organizations. And their lives ended in assassination. But the organized political movements to which they had contributed have moved on, from the interrogations and assassinations of their partisans, to engage in another discursive arrangement with their adversaries, that of negotiations – and eventual electoral participation and state formation. Depending on its definitions, colonialism was a matter of one or two centuries, although that time line is writ still in decisive ways across the global political cartography. Decolonization was even shorter-lived, but no less determining in the outlining of new geographies of struggle. From the documentary commitments and international testaments that followed two world wars and their adjudications to the "rights of small nations" and self-determination for colonized peoples, there has ensued at the end of the twentieth century a conflicted contest among the national and popular contenders over issues of sovereignty, developmentalism, cultural integrity, environmental protection and human rights more generally.

According to Article 22 of the Covenant of the League of Nations, created after the First World War, the "well-being and development" of the peoples in former enemy territories should form a "sacred trust of civilization." That criterion of a "sacred trust," following the Second World War was carried over into the Charter of the United Nations in 1945, and written into Chapter XI, Article 73, which reads:

> Members of the United Nations which have or assume responsibilities for the administration of territories whose peoples have not yet attained a full measure of self-government recognize the principle that the interests of the inhabitants of these territories are paramount, and accept as a sacred trust the obligation to promote to the utmost, within the system of international peace and security established by the present Charter, the well-being of the inhabitants of these territories.

To that end, it was further enjoined that the culture of those peoples would be protected, self-government would be developed and constructive measures of development encouraged. A decade later, in 1955, the final communiqué from the Asian–African Conference in Bandung that established the Non-Aligned Movement declared, with regard to the "Problems of Dependent Peoples," the agreement of its participants and signatories:

a. in declaring that colonialism in all its manifestations is an evil which should speedily be brought to an end;
b. in affirming that the subjection of peoples to alien subjugation, domination and exploitation constitute a denial of fundamental human rights, is contrary to the Charter of the United Nations and is an impediment to the promotion of world peace and co-operation;
c. in declaring its support of the cause of freedom and independence for all such peoples; and
d. in calling upon the powers concerned to grant freedom and independence to such peoples.

Those same issues of culture, self-government and development that had been so precisely identified by the various and sundry international covenants and documents still litter the terrain of political struggle and have ever since forced the reworkings of geopolitical priorities and human rights, even as the legacies of colonialism, decolonization and their global contests are renegotiated. Like the Indian sapper Kip in the British army in the Second World War, in Michael Ondaatje's 1993 novel *The English Patient*, the critics of the new geographies of struggle traverse a landscape and culture still strewn with the landmines and blasting caps of erstwhile conflicts:

> He had approached the villa on that night of the storm not out of curiosity about the music but because of the danger to the piano player. The retreating army often left pencil mines within musical instruments. Returning owners opened up pianos and lost their hands. People would revive the swing on a grandfather clock, and a glass bomb would blow out half a wall and whoever was nearby . . . He was unable to look at a room or field without seeing the possibilities of weapons there. (p. 75)

From Kanafani's "celebration of the skies" and airplane hijackings, then, to the unearthing of landmines across the globe, from the death sentence executed against Dalton to capital punishment and the international tribunals and world courts adjudicating the atrocities of "ethnic cleansing," from First's appeal for United Nations intervention in the case of South West Africa to the political mendacities of embargoes, sanctions and economic boycotts as putative foreign policy, the "new geographies of struggle" importantly represent the transformations and reversals that have resulted from the peripeties of the historic move – political, discursive, critical – from interrogation and assassination to negotiation. What was once written as "resistance literature" is discovering still other, alternative narrative possibilities in the paradigmatic contradictions on the grounds of human rights' reporting.

Writing Human Rights

Human rights reporting, itself a genre in the contemporary world of writing and rights, entails both documentation and intervention. A recording of facts and events, of abuses of individual

lives and national histories, as well as an effort to correct an official record that has systematically obscured those abuses, the
writing of human rights draws of necessity on conventions of
narrative and auto/biography, of dramatic representation and
discursive practices. Indeed, the thirty articles of the Universal
Declaration of Human Rights that was proclaimed by the
General Assembly of the United Nations in December 1948
translated the standard literary paradigm of individual versus
society and the narrative practices of plot and closure, by mapping an identification of the individual within a specifically
international construction of rights and responsibilities. The
Declaration can be read as recharting, for example, the trajectory
and peripeties of the classic *bildungsroman*. While that
Declaration has, since its adoption, been as much abused as used
by governments throughout the world, peoples and their representatives continue to appeal to its principles. It is those written
appeals, the reports of human rights monitors, the documentation of international organizations such as Amnesty
International, and the narratives of individuals in their efforts to
reconstruct a human history together with their readers' reconstructions, that might begin to form the basis of a discussion of
the relationships between writing and human rights, and the
place of a new body of literature, the active intersection of the
cultural and the political, in a changing contemporary international order.

Human Rights, Postmodernism and Observer Status

On 9 December 1993, Pierre Sane, Secretary General of Amnesty
International, addressed an audience gathered at the London
School of Economics. The occasion was International Human
Rights Day, commemorating the passage on 10 December 1948
by the United Nations of the Universal Declaration of Human
Rights. Sane's topic nearly half a century later was "human rights
in the 1990s: an agenda for action." His remarks both casti-
gated the continuing abuse of human rights worldwide and
without national exception, and bespoke the reasons for hope

that progress in the eradication of such abuse had begun and could still – eventually – be achieved. "Today," observed Sane, "human rights are almost always on the agenda in international relations. This would have seemed Utopian almost half a century ago." But if the call for the respect for human rights does indeed appear on such agendas, such calls all too often end in their own rhetorical ring, far short of any actual implementation, or otherwise serve covertly to ratify further abuses in the name of their own appeal. Sane thus argued that:

> [t]he question for us, therefore, is to develop a global counter-movement to protect all the rights of all the people from the global trends that threaten to destroy the very fabric of society in many countries. I believe that we need a new paradigm in which "substantive participation" – at local, national and international levels – is the primary goal, not an afterthought. It should integrate the values emerging from the human rights and other social movements, that are developing worldwide. It should put the human being back as the subject of history.

Such an argument as that proposed by Pierre Sane, for a "global counter-movement," for a "new paradigm of substantive participation," that would "put the human being back as the subject of history," would seem to ignore the dominant overdeterminations of an era identified differently by many cultural critics and theorists as "postmodern," an age thus characterized by "fragmentation, ephemerality, discontinuity and chaotic change" (Harvey, 1990, p. 44), disallowing too the effectiveness of human agency in plotting another historical narrative. But Sane, who had assumed leadership of AI only the previous year, has consistently maintained his contemporary – if un-postmodern – and urgent call for "global mobilization" on behalf of human rights. In his opening statement to the National Press Club in Washington DC on 20 October 1993, Sane went on to announce that "[w]e are here today to confront governments head on about what we see as one of the greatest threats to human rights in the 1990s. Murder and kidnapping at the hands of the state." He concluded his address with the admonition describing the "action Amnesty will be taking, the real cost of impunity, and the experience of people on the ground when confronted with 'disappearances' and political killings. Together, we are determined not to let governments get away with murder." In addition, then, to the imperative of restoring the "human being as the subject of history," Sane also argued the necessity of accountability of such subjects, against the impunity that governments grant to themselves and their agents, whether in Argentina following the investigation of mass *desapariciós* during that country's military dictatorship, in El Salvador when President Cristiani rejected the recommendations of the UN's Truth Commission Report in March 1993 on the abuses committed during the "decade of terror," and elsewhere. Against the prescriptions – and proscriptions – of postmodernism, Sane was insisting on the responsibility of the critic to observe, report and participate.

AI's new Secretary General, himself a Senegalese, similarly appealed to the representatives of the Organization of African Unity at its meeting on 25 June 1993. The OAU, he maintained, "must seize the initiative on human rights in Africa and adopt a bold, high-profile program for action to promote and protect human rights in our continent." In speaking to the OAU, Sane had only just left the convenings in Vienna that same month of the United Nations Conference on Human Rights at which the various received political mappings of the globe – East/West, North/South, even First/Second/Third worlds – had been significantly realigned as governments versus NGOs (non-governmental organizations). Although only official representatives of governments were allowed to present resolutions, cases, or issues and concerns before the assemblage, or to participate in the drafting of the conference's final resolutions, no government could itself be mentioned by name, whether as defending or defiling the human rights of its own or other citizens. While some countries, such as China, Indonesia, Syria and Iraq, did argue the issue of national sovereignty as taking precedence over human rights priorities, maintaining that the very discourse of human rights was a renewed form of cultural imperialism, NGOs such as AI or the victims themselves were not allowed a voice at the official deliberations. Speaking midway through the sessions then, on 21 June 1993, at the simultaneously held extracurricular meeting of the World

Conference on Human Rights, Pierre Sane condemned the proceedings as a "week of shame": It had been, he said:

> a week of political arrests. A week of abductions. A week of 'disappearances.' A week of torture. A week of political killings. And the people who have the torturers and the killers on their payroll were here in Vienna mouthing phrases about human rights. Almost half the governments of the world spoke at the conference. Their speeches added up to almost half a million words. But there is no evidence that any of those words saved a single life. There is no evidence that a single order was given to stop the torture and killing. Instead, they have turned this conference into a meeting about words rather than lives.

Postmodernism, perhaps – and in other words. Postmodernism, as many of both its protagonists and antagonists would concur, has a history of just such operations, "about words rather than lives."

Nearly half a century ago, the UN passed the Universal Declaration of Human Rights. Just over a quarter of a century ago, Malcolm X, in the last speech before his assassination in February 1965, proposed that

> [a]ll the nations that signed the charter of the UN came up with the Declaration of Human Rights and anyone who classifies his grievances under the label of 'human rights' violations can then be brought into the United Nations and be discussed by people all over the world. For as long as you call it "civil rights" your only allies can be the people in the next community, many of whom are responsible for your grievance. But when you call it "human rights" it becomes international. And then you can take your troubles to the World Court. You can take them before the world. And anybody anywhere on this earth can become your ally. Malcolm X, 1989, pp. 180–81

The universal fragmentation of postmodernism or the global mobilization of regional resistance on behalf of human rights? Can anybody anywhere on this earth still become your ally?

New Geographies of Struggle

"Postmodernism" in the current critical vernacular is often associated with the rhetoric of postcolonialism, a rhetoric which
postulates a narrative linearizing of the eras of colonialism and
postcolonialism. Such a narrative, however, in turn raises the
conundrums of sequentiality, historicity and periodization. Are
the historiographical debates raised, for example, by the rise of
postcolonialism as an academic "area of study", themselves the
consequence of a lexical detour? Has postcolonialism, as some
critics have suggested, always already been colonialism (see for
example Ashcroft, Griffiths and Tiffin, 1989)? Or is the very
area of alleged inquiry a misnomer, if not an anachronism?
Colonialism under another name? Or a precipitous invention of
a new disciplinary distortion? Can other narrative lines suggest
alternative investigations? Part of former US president George
Bush's rationale for the 1990–91 Gulf War was what was then
described (and has since been regularly invoked) as a "new
world order." That "new world order" occasions, however,
what might be determined in contrast as "new geographies of
struggle."[1] Beyond the more global analysis, there is no less
the remapping of the West/East conflict (however that may be
identified: as US/USSR or occidentalism/orientalism) as a
North/South confrontation. Such local reconstructions continue
as the erstwhile division of the world into First, Second, Third
arenas is refashioned in disequilibrated contests between the
remaining First World and the "two-thirds world" (Seabrook,
1993, p. 9). Nationalism is in its own turn become variously
absorbed by discussions of sub-, supra-, trans-, and multi-
nationalisms. And the intellectual commitment to
internationalism has devolved instead into the vogue of cos-
mopolitanism. The awkward nominations of developing
countries are resolved in naming emerging markets, and, more
academically, area studies are redefined (and refunded) as
regional trading blocs. The alleged threats to the world's order
have been variously designated accordingly, from (Islamic) fundamentalism to International Monetary Fundamentalism. And
resistance, too, once a name for an alternative to hegemony,
seems to have undergone its own lexical itinerary, in the

transition from national liberation to non-governmental organization. And an even longer term global project that was once magnificently exonerated in the name of a "civilizing mission" now goes, perhaps, under the exculpations of a "humanitarian intervention."

The biographies and bibliographies of Kanafani, Dalton and First, and their intersection with the organizational histories of the Palestinian, Salvadoran and South African struggles, are discovering new challenges across these new geographies of struggle and their lexical revisions.

To Talk or Not to Talk . . .

In response to the question of "Who killed Los Angeles?" – before as well as after the insurrections that took place following the now infamous verdict in the 1992 Rodney King trial – Mike Davis (1993) pointed to the "Webster doctrine of 'rapid containment'" as a means of waging a Kitsonian low-intensity war of counter-insurgency in the cities of the United States. Eschewing the "detective's function" in investigating this urban "assassination," Davis proposes instead the larger and more probing argument that "[t]his *Ulsterization*' of riot control in the inner city has an ominous, populist counterpart in the creeping *Israelization*' of residential security in affluent and valley districts" (p. 32, emphasis added).

But the PLO, like the ANC in South Africa and the FMLN in El Salvador – if not, for the moment, Sinn Fein as well – has gone on to engage in the process of negotiating a new set of political terms with their former foes on the battlefield of street strategy and armed struggle. Following more than four years of public/official negotiations with the apartheid government in South Africa, the ANC participated in, and won, popular elections in April 1994 – elections that, despite continued police and sectarian violence and questions of counting and accounting, they succeeded in carrying overwhelmingly. What would Ruth First have said? The FMLN as well, having become a legal political party (that has since disaggregated) subsequent to the peace accords with El Salvador's ARENA government signed in February 1992 and the official ceasefire in December of that same year, contested similar elections in March 1994. What would Roque Dalton have said? And on 13 September 1993, a photogenic handshake between PLO chairman Yasser Arafat and Israeli prime minister Yitzhak Rabin, overseen by President Clinton on the White House lawn, initiated the "declaration of principles," otherwise less euphemistically termed the "Gaza Jericho First" agreement, a title in which the territorial limitations of Gaza and Jericho negate the temporal promise and prospect of a future noted by "first." What would Ghassan Kanafani have said?

Each of these accords crucially involved – by both commission and omission – the controversial issues of "policing" and human rights. As the prominent Israeli commentator Israel Shahak, among others, has pointed out, the Israel–PLO agreement is itself grounded in the issue of policing: "the real meaning of the Oslo Agreement as Israel perceives it [is that] the PLO, or rather the part of Fatah with an absolute loyalty to Yasser Arafat, is intended to fulfill the role which the notables performed under Dayan and 'Village Leagues' under Sharon, but even more efficiently" (Shahak Report 125, 10 September 1993; see also *Middle East Report* editorial, November/December 1993). In South Africa, by contrast, the ANC refused to participate in the state police forces until it had attained power of its own in the country's government; and in El Salvador, too, the FMLN made the issue of "policing" central to their negotiations. A National Civilian Police (PNC) was created, and participation presumed to be barred now to former members of the armed forces and guerrillas alike who have been implicated in abuses against the Salvadoran people.

The uncritical assent, then, to the task of policing its own popular struggle on the part of Arafat's PLO – and unlike its counterparts in South Africa and El Salvador – suggests an abridgement of its former historic vision of a secular state and a democratic social order. Indeed, as the editors of *News From Within*, published in West Jerusalem, have pointed out in their analysis of the terms of the agreement, "[i]f there is an increase in nationalist incidents against settlers and other Israelis, and the Palestinian security forces fail to eradicate the violence, the Palestinian political leadership in Gaza and Jericho may take drastic steps to control the situation, and increasingly limit freedom, repress the opposition, and forbid them to express themselves. In this manner, *the first Palestinian experiment in independence could turn into a police state"* (*News From Within*, p. ix, 10, 5 October 1993, emphasis added).

Human rights, however, had no place at all in the Israel–PLO agreement, and the Palestine Human Rights Information Center, like Amnesty International and other observers, has expressed concern in this regard, calling for 1. a mechanism for redress for past Israeli gross and systematic abuses; 2. the incorporation of human rights mechanisms in state building; 3. human rights provisions for internal security officials; and 4. a national independent human rights commission (*News From Within*, p. ix, 10, 5 October 1993). While the UN Truth Commission's findings in El Salvador were almost immediately annulled by President Cristiani when he issued a decree of amnesty and impunity for the culprits – most of whom were from his own government and military. In South Africa, the ANC initiated an investigation into the allegations of abuses in its own concentration camps, and publicly admitted responsibility for serious abuses. AI applauded this accountability, but regretted the ANC's reluctance to prosecute the violators in its ranks until the South African government made similar acknowledgements and pursued parallel prosecutions.

Commenting then on the award of the 1993 Nobel Peace Prize to F. W. De Klerk and Nelson Mandela (an interesting parallel to those other dual recipients Anwar Sadat and Menachem Begin in 1978), AI maintained that

> in marked contrast to the government, the ANC has accepted responsibility for these abuses and has held two high-level commissions of inquiry into its own human rights record. Nevertheless, the ANC still needs to go further in acting on the recommendations of the inquiries. The South African government, meanwhile, still refuses to admit the scale of the violations committed by its own forces: despite clear evidence of their involvement in torture and assassinations, very few security force

officers have ever been brought to justice for human rights violations. (AI, 15 October 1993)

Kanafani had argued in the years before his death, perhaps
fatally, that a democratic secular state must be prepared for by a
democratic struggle – much as First had maintained a political
critique of directions and directives within her own movement,
and Dalton had contested the dictates of his organization. Two
decades later, their co-strategists, in El Salvador, in South Africa,
in Northern Ireland too, and elsewhere, are still confronted by
the newly conflicted imperatives of state-formation. Albie Sachs
has maintained that the question of rights is quintessential to a
future South Africa. In his book-length analysis of the question,
Protecting Human Rights in the New South Africa (1990d),
Sachs also critiques the development narrative of human rights:

> Most proponents of a Bill of Rights for South Africa operate
> within a thematically limited and historically out of date per-
> spective. Very few get beyond what has been called the first
> generation of rights, namely, civil and political rights and rights
> of due process, as were declared during the great anti-feudal and
> anti-colonial revolutions of the eighteenth century. The second
> generation of rights, namely those of a social, economic, and cul-
> tural nature enunciated in the United Nations Charter of Human
> Rights of the 1960s, get scant mention. The third generation of
> rights, the rights to development, peace, social identity, and a
> clean environment, which have been clearly identified as human
> and people's rights only in the past decade, get virtually no atten-
> tion at all. (pp. 7–8)

Against this developmental teleology, Sachs proposes what Kader
Asmal, also a member of the ANC Constitutional Committee
and now a cabinet minister whose portfolio is forestry and water
affairs, has "felicitously called blue rights, red rights, and green
rights. Each has its own sphere, its own modalities of enforcement; each has a fundamental and irreducible character, but all
need to be taken together in framing a constitution" (p. 9).

To talk or not to talk? The terms remain crucial.
"Ulsterization"? "Israelization"? Can the ANC and the FMLN

maintain their negotiating positions on democratic process? Will the Palestinians recover their own historic commitments? And what examples do they set for a changing (but, all that notwith-standing, perhaps hardly new) world order?

. . . from Interrogation to Negotiation

A broad spectrum of stalwart Fatah militants have received their matriculation credentials in Israeli jails. One of them once told me that he considered it unfortunate that Yasser Arafat had not spent some years of his life in an Israeli jail. This might have dis-inclined him from all his frivolous gestures. Perhaps one could on this occasion go into a non-conventional thinking farther. For years we regretted the generosity we had showed in 1985 when we had released hundreds of veteran terrorist [sic] prisoners in exchange for a handful of our POW's. Now, when Israel's hopes are pinned no longer on Arafat and his clique of mercenary politi-cians, but rather on former prisoners and deportees from the Israeli occupation, we could permit ourselves to think that the tragedy had also its somewhat brighter side. (Shahak Report 140, 24 June 1994)

These remarks, witting or unwitting, from the Israeli commen-tator Nahum Barnea cited by Israel Shahak in his June 1994 report on "the first weeks of autonomy" in the designated areas of Palestinian political rule in Jericho and the Gaza Strip – and their own cynicism, even fallacies, perhaps hypocrisy, notwith-standing – identify a critical narrative that has developed from out of the period of decolonization and in what has since been referred to as the new age of "postcolonialism." Indeed, it was only in 1988, in the early days of the Palestinian intifada, that Israeli officials had been regretting that same 1985 prisoner exchange and the political reorganization it had enabled, much as in early 1995 the subsequent policy of deportation of Palestinian activists to Lebanon seemed to be having direly neg-ative consquences in the Hamas and Islamic Jihad bombing campaigns against Israeli targets.

The role played by political detention, however, in the

schooling and disciplining of cadres and leaders alike in the national liberation organizations and resistance movements has been given new imperatives in the emergent state-building and nation formation projects of those erstwhile struggles. But while these transitions at the end of the twentieth century have been rhetorically recognized and even rewarded by such international accolades as the Nobel Peace Prize – first to Nelson Mandela and F. W. De Klerk in 1993 and then, in 1994, to Yitzhak Rabin and Yasser Arafat – their significance requires more specific and conditioned scrutiny and discriminating rehabilitations. Pointing to the differences made by political prison and detention, Edward Said has argued (in a much circulated citation) against that very analogy suspectly created by the Nobel commission: argued, that is, that while Nelson Mandela remained in prison for twenty-seven years to liberate South Africa, it was the Palestinian people themselves who spent twenty-seven years under occupation in order to liberate Yasser Arafat. The transition, in other words, from "interrogation" to "negotiation" enjoins an important relearning of the determinations of political discourse and the options of political power.

While in South Africa, for example, former Robben Island detainees fulfill (albeit in varying degrees of capability) their new roles as government ministers, members of parliament, even as president of the "new South Africa," no less than as partisans in the ANC in its renewed function as political party outside the government, Palestinian long-time ex-prisoners in December 1994 gathered in Gaza to engage in a roundtable discussion of "what happened to the dream?" That discussion, reported in the West Jerusalem-based publication *News from Within* (p. xi, 1, January 1995), was itself encumbered by continuing restrictions on the movement of Palestinians and border closures under the ongoing Israeli occupation of the rest of the territories. What further emerged from the roundtable meeting, however, was itself another kind of negotiation, the critical engagement of the former prisoners from across the several PLO factions (and whose collective and individual fates had not been included in the negotiations that resulted in the Oslo and Cairo agreements) with the newly established Palestinian Authority under the control of Yasser Arafat and his Fatah followers. For Adnan Rahman

Shalaldeh (PFLP), it was as if "as people who participated in the struggle, our role had been marginalized," and that he felt now "like a stranger in this situation" (p. 4). According to Ibrahim Said Muhammad Sheikha (FIDA), then, "We should avoid the factionalization and deal with each other on a common basis; on the basis of the 'prisoner community'" (p. 5). Shalaldeh responded to his former fellow prisoner that "the question is: how should we deal with the Authority?" (p. 5). And Ghazi Abu Jiyab (PFLP) later remarked that the "alternative is to define the relationship between the Authority and the opposition by other means" (p. 12). What, however, would those other means be? For Abu Jiyab, "Even the occupation didn't act like Abu Ammar [Arafat] did in closing the newspaper *An-Nahar* last summer. Abu Ammar is dealing with Rabin like we used to deal with the head of the prison administration. We used to put forth a number of requests and we would say, '*Bevakasha* [Please] this is what we want,' and he would look into them and decide" (p. 12).

The historic transposition from interrogation to negotiation is fraught with the reciprocal relocation of speaking roles and a radical redistribution of discursive powers. According to Ghassan Kanafani, long since assassinated in 1972 by the Israeli Mossad, the ideals of a democratic secular state could only be achieved through a democratic revolution, and it is that revolution itself that is being re-examined now, more than two decades later, through the optic of the terms of the Oslo and Cairo agreements and under the conditions of the Palestinian Authority and the frustrated "peace process," a process that Dan Connell (1995) has otherwise appraised as the "'privatization' of the occupation" (pp. 6–9). Such a revisioning across a divide riven by new geographies of struggle (or, more cynically, a "new world order") is not without its parallels within other movements in other parts of the formerly colonized world: in South Africa as the ANC engages with the impositions of statecraft; in El Salvador, where the FMLN has again divided itself after being forced to contend with parliamentary procedures even as the military and its paramilitary collaborators continued their campaign of death threats and assassination; and, perhaps if only anticipatorily, in Northern Ireland, following the IRA ceasefire of September 1994 and Sinn Fein's awkward approach to a seat at

the negotiating table – so desperately interrupted. With Arafat
and Mandela as potential locutory political models, the Sinn
Fein leadership has been indeed on notice as to the imperilled
consequences of the conflicted transpositions from interrogation
to negotiation. What would Ghassan Kanafani, Roque Dalton
and Ruth First have had to say?

The question *in extremis* for political detainees of "when to
talk and when not to talk," and their respective movements'
larger strategic and tactical issues of secrecy, clandestinity and
intelligence, assumes in the circumstances of negotiation necessarily new and alternative directives and directions. From the
brutal interrogative inquiries described in his prison memoir *Cage
Eleven* to the public relations interlocutions of the *Larry King
Show* on CNN or a Saint Patrick's Day occasion at the White
House, Gerry Adams, for example, has had not only to rearticulate his speech patterns but to refigure his speaking partners.
Once ostracized for talking at all with the IRA, Adams was then
celebrated as someone who can – and must – do precisely that:
talk to the IRA, even as he is paradoxically called upon to insist
on the decommissioning of IRA arms, if not the organizational
dissolution of the IRA itself. In South Africa, the ANC remains a
political party outside the government, insisting on the need to
maintain the critical space that it had so radically created during
the more than forty years of struggle against apartheid. In El
Salvador, however, the FMLN's split has dramatically raised the
issue of the life history and historical narrative, the continuities
and closures, beginnings, middles and ends, so to speak, of
national liberation and resistance. In the Israeli-occupied
Palestinian territories, the question of the status of the state, the
contradictions between that formula "agreed" upon and the one
that had once been envisioned, are riddling the narrative of liberation. As former prisoner Ibrahim Said Muhammad Sheikha
(FIDA), speaking during the Gaza roundtable, described the difficult transition from interrogation to negotiation:

> My biggest concern is the sector called "the prisoners," and espe-
> cially those old-timers who spent their youth in prisons. We were
> denied higher education, we were unable to build a financial nest
> egg or to form families. We were excluded from the history that

the rest of the society experienced. When we were released, society absorbed us, but our national and social institutions did not. I don't work at anything: no job, no office. I want to live in dignity. I don't want to extend my hand in need of anyone. I'm not looking for help from people, but I am concerned about the rest of my life as a freedom-fighter who is now 50 years old. I don't want anything in return. I only want to live a decent, normal life as a simple person.

Now I don't see the National Authority [PA] as being capable of guaranteeing our needs. So I work day in and day out on the prisoner issue. My wife was also a prisoner. I want prisoners to be insured and to be taken care of, whether they are in prison or out. I see the released prisoners in Jericho, how they have barbed wire around them and guards. Is this how we absorb prisoners, with watchdogs? Absorbing the freedom-fighter means returning him to society.

From interrogation to negotiation, to be sure, but then . . .? The personal biographies of former prisoners, like the liberation narratives to which they contributed, are critical to the rewriting of other national historiographies.

The Penalties of Death

The first law which it becomes a reformer to propose and support, at the approach of a period of great political change, is the abolition of the punishment of death.
Percy B. Shelley (cited in Peter Linebaugh, 1995)

Amnesty International USA (AIUSA) today called on President Clinton to strongly condemn China's "public order" executions in the weeks before the Fourth United Nations Conference on Women, due to convene August 30.
AIUSA release: 16 August 1995

Death squads, police guns, letter bombs and paramilitary units had once done much of the desperate work of suppressing political and cultural dissent, and eliminating alternative opinion. More lately, however, that work would seem to have become the dispensation of some select judicial systems in their enforcement of the death penalty. The survivors of the assassinations of their comrades and their colleagues have in the meantime made vociferous their opposition to this officialization of "assassination" as "capital punishment." For example, the international response was clearly coordinated and precisely articulated to the death warrant against Mumia Abu-Jamal signed in the late evening hours of 1 June 1995 by Pennsylvania governor Tom Ridge. On 2 June the ANC wrote a letter to the governor signed by its secretary general M. C. Ramaphosa, requesting the commutation of the death sentence. Nelson Mandela would later write a similar letter. Meanwhile, though, the ANC's June letter had been preceded by the protest of political prisoners internationally, in the United States, Germany, Italy, Denmark, Belgium, Chile, Peru, Spain, Canada, France, and by Irish prisoners in the United States. South African trade unions would join the campaign to save Mumia Abu-Jamal, and *An Phoblacht*, the Irish republican newspaper would advocate on his behalf, as would republican prisoners in the north of Ireland, as well as Assata Shakur, a former US political prisoner living now – following her escape (or "excarceration") from a US prison – in Cuba. And even as the US media remained throughout that summer almost unanimously silent on the issue of his sentence, mass demonstrations took place across the rest of the world on Abu-Jamal's behalf . . . until on 7 August, presiding Judge Sabo (infamous as the "hanging judge") was obliged to grant an indefinite stay of execution for the writer as he pursued his appeals through the judicial system. *Live from Death Row* (1995) is the title of Abu-Jamal's collection of the essays from his thirteen years on that row. His analyses both challenge the systemic abuses to which those who are not even allowed to "do time" are submitted and grant time – and time and a place – to those who have shared his space on death row. It is, after all, a *Race for Justice* (1995), as announced in the title to the work of Abu-Jamal's attorney, Leonard Weinglass, on his behalf – and against both political assassination and the death penalty which were reinstituted in the United States in 1977, reinstantiating once again that protracted history of "the rope, the chair, and the needle" (see Marquart, Ekland-Olson and Sorensen, 1994).

Writers and assassination – new geographies of struggle: the place – "death row;" and the time – a "race for justice"? The penalties of death are exacting a high price indeed from the body politic. As Ken Saro-Wiwa, the Nigerian activist and leader of Movement for the Survival of the Ogoni People (MOSOP), who was executed in November 1995, spoke in the opening to his "statement from the dock" to the Nigerian military-appointed special tribunal that condemned to death Saro-Wiwa and his colleagues:

> We all stand before history. I am a man of peace, of ideas. Appalled by the denigrating poverty of my people who live on a richly endowed land, distressed by their political marginalization and economic strangulation, angered by the devastation of their land, their ultimate heritage, anxious to preserve their right to life and to a decent living, and determined to usher to this country as a whole a fair and just democratic system which protects everyone and every ethnic group and gives us all a valid claim to human civilization, I have devoted my intellectual and material resources, my very life, to a cause in which I have total belief and from which I cannot be blackmailed or intimidated.

Meanwhile, Amnesty International, Human Rights Watch and other non-governmental human rights organizations argued the imperative of the establishment of an international court that would oversee the continued abuses of power by states and their appointees, colonial and postcolonial, as well as the new assaults on individual and collective struggles for justice. Like AI, HRW advocated the establishment of a "permanent International Criminal Court, available to try human rights criminals wherever national judicial systems fail to do so" (Press Release, 7 December 1995).

Commissions of Truth

The time is the present and the place, a country that is probably Chile, but could be any country that has given itself a democratic government just after a long period of dictatorship.
Ariel Dorfman, *Death and the Maiden* (Setting), 1991

Death and the Maiden, by the Chilean writer and dramatist Ariel Dorfman, represents provocatively the contradictions and limitations to the establishing and the mandated work of "truth commissions," those new bodies of inquiry, set up in countries that have, whether through military victory or negotiated settlement, entered into a transition period from one form of regime (often described as a "dictatorship") to another system of rule and rules (just as often identified as a "democracy"). Dorfman's three-act play has three characters: Paulina, a victim of torture and interrogation who has survived her ordeal to marry eventually her former colleague in the opposition, Gerardo; Gerardo, who did not undergo the same tests as his wife, but who has that day been named by the president of that unnamed country to head its "truth commission," investigating human rights violations from the past; and, finally, Roberto Miranda, who has just that night assisted Gerardo in repairing a flat tire on his car, but who, in the past, it seems, participated in perpetrating those very violations that Gerardo has been presidentially assigned to investigate, and that Paulina has suffered. Dorfman's play, which has been performed in theaters from London to Johannesburg, and remade as a film with Roman Polanski as its director, argues painfully the several sides to such a commission of truth. Paulina, for example, challenges her husband – and the commission's eventual chairperson – with its own mandate: "This Commission that you've been appointed to," she says. "Doesn't it only investigate cases that ended in death?" (p. 6). Gerardo can only acquiesce in her critique of his assignment, "Limited, let's say we're limited" (p. 7). But Miranda (whose very name might well contain an allusive reference to the US "Miranda rights" and the right to remain silent under questioning to protect the interrogated against incrimination), suggests that perhaps Gerardo might well rework his commitments: "Instead of proposing dishonourable solutions to me, you should be out there convincing that madwoman of yours to cease this criminal behaviour before she ruins your brilliant career and ends up in gaol or in an asylum. Tell her that. Or can't you impose a little order in your own house?" (p. 38). In public and in private, Gerardo's later reply suggests the complications of truth commissions: "I'm tired of being in the middle of this. You reach an understanding with her, you convince her" (p. 40).

"In the middle of this," as Gerardo describes it, has been alternatively formulated as "justice in transition," the problem, that is, of dealing with the past as part of establishing grounds for the present and making way for the future. Dorfman's play was published in 1990, the same year that the Report of the Chilean Commission on Truth and Reconciliation carried out its work of investigating the assaults on human rights by the military dictatorship that took power following the brutal overthrow of Salvador Allende's Popular Unity government in September 1973. According to Supreme Decree No. 355, issued by Chilean president Aylwin's new government on 25 April 1990, there was created a Commission of Truth and Reconciliation, with a mandate as wide-reaching as it was limited. According to Article One of the Bill, the work was to be carried out "without, however, affecting any legal proceedings to which those events might give rise;" the names of the victims would be provided, but the identification of the perpetrators would be concealed; and, much as Paulina dramatically worried, only "serious violations" would be investigated. Again, according to Article One, "serious violations" were to be understood as "situations of those persons who disappeared after arrest, who were executed, or were tortured to death, in which the moral responsibility of the state is compromised as a result of actions by its agents or persons in its service, as well as kidnappings and attempts on the lives of persons committed by private citizens for political purposes" (p. 6). The description of "serious violations," in other words, could not be presented by those who had suffered them. For they were gone – whether disappeared, deceased, assassinated . . . they were gone.

The report by Chile's "truth commission," delivered in 1991, followed on three Latin American precedents: the investigation carried out by the Argentine Commission on the Disappeared (1984), whose title *Nunca Más* provided as well the watchword for subsequent inquiries; Brazil's *Nunca Mais* (1985); and then, in 1989, Uruguay's investigation under the same denomination. For all that these publications were able to report on the recent national histories of their governments, questions remained, questions that generate further discussion. What is the relation between decrees of amnesty and adjudications of justice? Beyond "truth," and its determinations, what must yet be sought? An acknowledgement – or admission, even confession – on the part of those responsible? Should there be reparations for the victims – and/or their families? And as for those deemed responsible for the most serious of abuses, what limits should be set on their eventual responsibilities? Indeed, should prosecution and punishment of the perpetrators follow on the findings of "truth commissions"? What of pardons and amnesties and impunities?

In Argentina, the National Commission on the Disappeared, headed by Ernesto Sabato, had been constituted by the newly elected president Alfonsín, and had the support of the country's government – although the military junta responsible for the near decade of Argentina's "dirty war" had destroyed most of its security files prior to their departure from the governing halls. Brazil's report, by contrast, was undertaken during the terror itself, and was sponsored by the Church in that country; the security files were available to the investigators, albeit not without the difficulties imposed by the continued need for secrecy and clandestinity. The Uruguayan researchers, in the preface to their own documentary, acknowledged these precedents: "Argentinians and Brazilians both saw the need to write and publish a report that would make *Nunca Más* sound loud and clear in their countries. In Argentina, the investigations were carried out with government support; in Brazil, they were carried out with the support of the church. But in Uruguay neither the government nor the church provided a *Nunca Más* report. A few individual researchers attempted to do so, but they were overcome by the difficulty of the task. As a result, Servicio Paz y Justicia, Peace and Justice Service (SERPAJ) took on the job" (p. vii). And in Chile, according to Jose Zalaquett's preface to the English language edition of the report, and responding to these other examples, it had become now the "positive duty of successor governments to dispense justice for past crimes," a duty that was of a "different nature than the negative obligation of refraining from committing them" (p. xxviii). Or as Zalaquett would otherwise tell a conference in South Africa in February 1994 on that same critical topic of "justice in transition," "It is one thing for human rights organizations to be above the fray of politics in the face of a dictatorial government, but to do so in a political transition is a different matter" (Boraine, Levy and Scheffer, 1994, p. 9).

A very different matter indeed. Within days of the publication in March 1993 of the report of the United Nations Truth Commission on twelve years of war in El Salvador, then president Alfredo Cristiani officially pardoned all those implicated in the atrocities of the previous decade. "Beware of the words 'amnesty' and 'reconciliation'," Tina Rosenberg had told the participants in the 1994 conference in South Africa. And indeed, despite the concerted recommendations to the contrary, the agents who had committed the abuses chronicled in that report on El Salvador, entitled in Spanish *De la locura a la esperanza* (*From madness to hope*), would go on to indulge their impunity by continuing as members of the government, officers in the military, and functionaries in the country's various bureaucratic apparatuses. The Truth Commission's report, however, following upon a chronology of the years of violence, had proceeded to examine specific cases of the violence, including – for some examples – the army killings of peasants and villagers in El Mozote (1981), at the Rio Sumpul (1980), of members of unions (FENASTRAS) and human rights organizations (COMADRES) (1989), to the death squad killings of Archbishop Romero (1980), and the army's assassinations of Ignacio Ellacuría and his fellow Jesuits with their housekeeper and her young daughter (1989). And while Cristiani saw fit to amnesty the parties to these deaths who had been identified in the Truth Commission's report, the United States government (which in many cases had provided the training, and funding, for those very parties) saw partially fit to take some issue with the commission's findings. As Representative Robert Torricelli (NJ) wrote to his colleague Lee Hamilton, chair of the House's Committee on Foreign Affairs, in the letter of transmittal that accompanied the report on the "comparison of US Administration Testimony and Reports with the 1993 UN Truth Commission Report on El Salvador":

The CRS [Congressional Research Service] shows a disturbing pattern of administration deception with respect to the human

rights violations investigated by the Truth Commission. In several cases, administration testimony before Congress tended to:
- attribute more political violence to the guerrillas than the facts warranted;
- attribute right-wing violence to unspecified right-wing elements independent of the government, while absolving the government of responsibility;
- attribute to combat operations deaths that were known to be due to massacres; and
- dismiss contrary information as guerrilla-inspired. (5 March 1993)

In particular, the disagreements involved the deaths of Archbishop Romero, the refugees at Rio Sumpul, the US churchwomen, the peasants at El Mozote, and the members of FENASTRAS and COMADRES. There might have been some residue of truth indeed in the telling.

Truth or justice remained the question in South Africa's deliberations concerning the investigation of the past apartheid government. Nontsikelelo Biko, for example, the widow of Steve Biko who died in police custody, demanded "justice, not amnesty" for those responsible for her husband's death (Reuters, 13 June 1995). She was speaking only a month before the signing by Nelson Mandela of a bill creating a commission to inquire into "apartheid-era crimes" (Reuters, 19 July 1995). That bill, the "Promotion of National Unity and Reconciliation Bill," proposed a manifold mandate for the constitutional commission that would be established, a mandate that called for "as complete a picture as possible" of the wrongs committed from 1 March 1960 on, the "granting of amnesty to persons who make full disclosure," the "affording [to] victims an opportunity to relate the violations they suffered," the "granting of reparation," and "recommendations aimed at the prevention of the commission of gross violations of human rights." Truth in the telling: the very project was daunting, not just for those for whose work had been explicitly in what Aryeh Neier described as "forms of abuse devised for purposes of deniability" (Boraine, Levy and Scheffer, 1994, p. 6), but for those former resistance fighters who had relied on secrecy and "not talking" to interrogators if the liberation struggle in which they were engaged was to sustain its mission. As the SACP had told its adherents in a document entitled "Secret Work," issued as part of the Umsebenzi series (1988–90):

> Secrecy gives us protection by starving the enemy of information about us. Secrecy helps us build a strong revolutionary movement to overthrow the enemy.
>
> There is nothing sinister about using secret methods to help win freedom. Through the ages the ruling classes have made it as difficult as possible for the oppressed people to gain freedom. The oppressors use the most cruel and sinister methods to stay in power. They use unjust laws to ban, banish, imprison and execute their opponents. They use secret police, soldiers, spies and informers against the people's movements. But the people know how to fight back and how to use secret methods of work.

And now again those same secrets must be made public, in the work of South Africa's Truth Commission, which had its first sitting in December 1995 with Bishop Desmond Tutu as its Chairman and Judge President. As Zakes Mofokeng, the South African playwright, wrote in the program notes to his new production, *Never Again*:

> I decided on this production after seriously thinking about the present situation in South Africa. We are all engaged in an exercise to bring about reconciliation, but reconciliation cannot come about by simply trying to forget and forgive. Now is the time for all those who were segregated to reveal themselves to each other, and get to know each other well. We must bring to light our feelings that were bottled up during those times of oppression. We must know each other so that we can understand each other and together start on the new road to the future. (program notes, Austin, TX, 1 December 1995)

There would, however, be no such an inquiry contained in the "Declaration of Principles" signed between Arafat's PLO and the Israeli government on 13 September 1993.[2] In that document, the articles dealt only with: 1. the aim of the negotiations;

2. the framework for the interim period; 3. elections; 4. jurisdiction; 5. the transitional period and permanent status negotiations; 6. preparatory transfer of powers and responsibilities; 7. an interim agreement; 8. public order and security; 9. laws and military orders; 10. a joint Israeli–Palestinian liaison committee; 11. Israeli–Palestinian cooperation in economic fields; 12. liaison and cooperation with Jordan and Egypt; 13. redeployment of Israeli forces; 14. Israeli withdrawal from the Gaza Strip and Jericho area; 15. resolution of disputes; and 16. Israeli–Palestinian cooperation concerning regional programs. Many critics, like criminology professor Stan Cohen, asked whether there even was place in such a "declaration of principles" for "truth and reconciliation." "Our transition," Cohen wrote in 1995:

> is unlike those in Latin America, Eastern Europe and South Africa in obvious ways. First the Oslo and Cairo agreements are inadequate for fulfilling Palestinian aspirations and providing for national rights. Second, the Israeli government is backtracking on even these provisions in humiliating ways. Third, all of the human rights violations from the "old days" continue in the West Bank and the edges of the autonomous areas: torture and ill-treatment of detainees (now Hamas rather than Fatah), house demolitions, restrictions of movement (more severe than ever before) and, above all, extrajudicial killings by IDF undercover units. Fourth, there are the unresolved questions about the legal implications of the Declaration of Principles: has the occupation, even in Gaza and Jericho, ended or merely redeployed? How has the dual legal system (one for Israelis, one for Palestinians) been perpetuated? Finally, and most importantly, there is the blatant expansion of settlements, confiscation of land, and the massive extension of Jerusalem's boundaries. (p. 4)

Occupation or separation? The Hebrew word for "separation" used by Yitzhak Rabin to describe the relation between the two peoples is an exact translation of the word "apartheid."

What would Ghassan Kanafani, Roque Dalton and Ruth First have had to say?

Our homeopath, speaking to Gillian, also said, "Your father has unfinished business; people with unfinished business don't die quickly."
Helena Dolny, Epilogue to *Slovo: The Unfinished Autobiography* (1995/6)

The chronologies – the commemorations and celebrations that they occasion – of world wars and national liberation struggles are writ boldly across the twentieth century, determining and overdetermining historical narratives and now new geographies of struggle. And it was across those very chronological terrains that Ghassan Kanafani, Roque Dalton and Ruth First worked and wrote, and which, in their writing, they sought to redraft into new arenas of cultural and political engagement.

The focus in the foregoing sketches of that writing, a limited concentration on the historical relationship of a writer/partisan to their work, as well as to the social and political order within which they live and write has been not so much in order to recuperate conventions of authorship or subjectivity as it has been to allow for an inquiry into the complex, often conflicted, position of the intellectual within the structures of a political party or organized resistance movement and to question their function as historical agents in actively challenging dominant, even oppressive, orders.

Can truth be committed in the telling? In exhuming corpses or in examining corpuses? The assassins – or at least their affiliations – of those responsible for the deaths of Ghassan Kanafani, Roque Dalton and Ruth First have all been identified and have even admitted to their deeds. But the projects of those writers' lives, terms and terminations, amnesty, dissent – against the continued paradigmatic sway of assassinations and death penalties – require still the work of commissions of truth. Their struggle, for popular liberation and truth in the telling, engages new political commitments, other cultural concerns, and new territories of critical inquiry.

Appendices

Ghassan Kanafani

born 1936/died 1972

Ghassan Kanafani, whose obituary in the Beirut *Daily Star* hailed him as "the commando who never fired a gun," was a critic, novelist and journalist. Born in Akka in 1936, Kanafani left in 1948 with the Palestinian refugees and grew up in Damascus where he was educated in the UNRWA schools. He began his writing and teaching career in Kuwait between 1956 and 1960 until returning to Beirut where he joined George Habash in the Arab Nationalist Movement (ANM). He later became a member of the Popular Front for the Liberation of Palestine (PFLP) and edited its journal *al-Hadaf* until his death in a car-bomb explosion in 1972. In addition to his novels such as *Men in the Sun*, *On Men and Guns*, and *Return to Haifa*, short stories, and plays, Kanafani authored three volumes of literary criticism. He was the first reader, in *Literature of Resistance in Occupied Palestine 1948–1966*, to apply the term "resistance literature" (*adab al-muqawama*) to Palestinian writing. His political essays, like the study of the 1936–39 revolt in Palestine, daily writings, and feature columns in the various Arab newspapers with which he was associated between 1961 and 1972 constitute a major contribution to modern Arab political thought and strategy.

Al-athar al-kamila (*Collected works*). In four volumes. Beirut:
  Dar al-Tali'a, 1972–1977.

NOVELS. Volume One (1972).
Rijal fi-l-shams (*Men in the Sun*) 1963.
Ma tabaqa lakum (*All That's Left to You*) 1966.
'Ai'd ila Haifa (*Return to Haifa*) 1969.
Um Sa'ad 1969.
Al-Ashaq (*The Lover*) unfinished.
Barquq Nissan (*April Anemones*) unfinished.

STORY COLLECTIONS. Volume Two (1973).
Maut sarir raqm 12 (*The Death of Bed Number 12*) 1961.
Ard al-burtuqal al-hazin (*The Land of Sad Oranges*) 1963.
'Alam laisa lana (*The World That Is Not Ours*) 1965.
'An rijal wa-l-banadiq (*On Men and Guns*) 1968.

DRAMA. Volume Three (1976).

LITERARY STUDIES. Volume Four (1977).
Adab al-muqawama fi Filastin al-muhtalla 1948–1966 (*Literature
  of Resistance in Occupied Palestine 1948–1966*) 1966.
Al-adab al-filastini al-muqawam taht al-ihtilal 1948–1968
  (*Palestinian Resistance Literature Under Occupation
  1948–1968*) 1968.
Fi-l-adab al-sihyuni (*On Zionist Literature*) 1967.

JOURNALISM/POLITICAL ESSAYS:
"Thoughts on Change and the 'Blind Language'", *Al-Hadaf*,
  919–920, 1988.
"The 1936–1939 Revolution in Palestine", *Shu'un Filastiniya*, 6,
  1972.
"On the Abu Hamidu Case and the Issue of Cultural
  'Cooperation' with the Enemy," *Shu'un Filastiniya*, 12,
  August 1972.
and additional essays in *Al-Hadaf*, *Al-Hurriya*, *Shu'un
  Filastiniya*, etc.
Al-Qandil al-saghir (*The Little Lamp*). Beirut and Cairo: Dar al-
  Fata al-Arabi, 1980 [children's story].

ENGLISH TRANSLATIONS:

Men in the Sun and Other Palestinian Stories. Translated by
   Hilary Kilpatrick. London: Heinemann and Washington DC:
   Three Continents Press, 1978.

Palestine's Children. Translated by Barbara Harlow. London:
   Heinemann, Cairo: Dar al-Fata al-Arabi, Washington DC:
   Three Continents Press, 1984.

All That's Left To You: A Novella and Other Stories. Translated
   by May Jayyusi and Jeremy Reed. Austin TX: Center for
   Middle Eastern Studies, 1990.

Roque Dalton

born 1935/died 1975

Roque Dalton, a Salvadoran poet and political theorist, was accused of collaboration with the CIA and executed in 1975 by members of the ERP, his own resistance organization, following internal schisms over the debates on the efficacy of militarism versus a "prolonged people's war" as the strategy demanded by El Salvador's historical and material circumstances. As a poet, he composed numerous volumes of poetry, including *Poemas clandestinas*, and a critique of poetry and the "bourgeois poet," *Poetry and Militancy in Latin America*. *Probrecita poeta que era yo . . .* narrates his own complex and conflicted relation to the activity of writing in the resistance, much as *Un libro rojo para Lenin* attempts to rework the political framework of that complicated activity. His response to Régis Debray's controversial *Revolution in the Revolution?*, entitled *¿Revolución en la revolución? y la critica de derecha*, challenged the orthodoxies of Latin American communism in the late 1960s to come to new practical and theoretical terms with the changed conditions of struggle. This volume, like his recording of the *testimonio* or oral history of Miguel Marmol and the 1932 massacre in El Salvador, are important contributions to the theorizing of resistance in the then Third World.

POETRY COLLECTIONS:

La ventana en el rostro. Mexico: Ediciones de Andrea, 1961.

Poemas clandestinas/Clandestine Poems. Translated by Jack Hirschman. Edited by Barbara Paschke and Eric Weaver. San Francisco: Solidarity Publications, 1984.

Taberna y otros lugares. Havana: Casa de las Americas, 1969.

Un libro levemente odioso. Mexico: La Letra Editores, 1988.

PROSE/ESSAYS:

"Poesia y Militancia en America Latina," *Casa de las Americas*, 20–21, September–December 1963.

Poetry and Militancy in Latin America. Willimantic, CT: Curbstone Press, 1981.

El Salvador (monografía). Havana: Casa de las Americas, 1963.

El intelectual y la sociedad (1969). Mexico City: Siglo XXI Editores, 1985.

¿Revolución en la revolución? *y la critica de derecha*. Havana: Casa de las Americas, 1970.

Miguel Marmol. 1971.

Miguel Marmol. Translated by Kathleen Ross and Richard Schaaf. Willimantic, CT: Curbstone Press, 1987.

Las historias prohibidas de pulgarcito. (1974) Mexico: Siglo XXI Editores, 1985.

Un libro rojo para Lenin. Managua: Editorial Nueva Nicaragua, 1986.

Probrecito poeta que era yo . . . Centroamerica: EDUCA, 1976.

Ruth First

born 1925/died1982

Ruth First was assassinated in 1982 by a parcel bomb, delivered to her at the Centre for African Studies, where she was a researcher at the Eduardo Mondlane University in Mozambique. As a journalist and political activist in the 1960s in South Africa, she had covered such stories as the exploitative conditions on the farms in the Transvaal for the successively suppressed publications the *Guardian*, *New Age*, *The Spark* and *Clarion*. (Her co-author of one investigative report, Joe Gqabi, was himself assassinated in exile in 1983.) In exile in England, she edited the manuscript of *South Africa: The Peasants' Revolt*, written by Govan Mbeki, the ANC leader sentenced to life imprisonment in the Rivonia Trial. Her last work, *Black Gold*, was a study of the Mozambican miner and peasant and combined historical analysis of migrant labor patterns with interviews and compilations of work songs and popular narratives from the miners and their families. Her other works include a study of the new regime of Gadafi, *Libya*; a history of army coups in Africa, *Political Power in Africa*; *South West Africa*; a literary biography of Olive Schreiner, co-authored with Ann Scott; and her own prison autobiography, *117 Days*. It was Ruth First, too, wife of the late Joe Slovo (who died in January 1995), leader of the South African

Communist Party and the ANC's armed wing, Umkhonto we Sizwe, who edited the collection of Nelson Mandela's speeches and writings, *No Easy Walk to Freedom*.

BOOKS:
South West Africa. Harmondsworth: Penguin, 1963.

117 Days. Harmondsworth: Penguin and New York: Stein & Day, 1965. Reprinted New York: Monthly Review Press, 1989.

The Barrel of a Gun: Political Power in Africa. London: Allen Lane, 1970. Reprinted as *Power in Africa: Political Power in Africa and the Coup d'Etat*. New York: Pantheon, 1970.

The South African Connection: Western Investment in Apartheid. With Jonathan Steele and Christabel Gurney. London: Temple Smith, 1972.

Libya: The Elusive Revolution. Harmondsworth: Penguin Books, 1974.

Olive Schreiner. With Ann Scott. London: André Deutsch, 1980.

Black Gold: The Mozambican Miner, Proletarian and Peasant. Sussex: The Harvester Press/New York: Saint Martin's Press, 1983.

For additional citations, see the bibliography compiled by Gavin Williams and available at the Institute of Commonwealth Studies; further references are to be found in the Ruth First Collection (RFC) at the Institute which contains materials and manuscripts from First's radio plays, selections of her journalism, and the correspondence related to her edited and co-edited work, as well as articles and encyclopedia entries, notes for lectures and talks, and conference presentations.

Notes

Part II   1 History and Endings: Ghassan Kanafani and the Politics of Terminations in Palestine

1. With appreciation to Farouq Ghandour for long ago (1983) sharing this observation.

Part II   2 *Habeas Corpus:* Roque Dalton and the Politics of Amnesty in El Salvador

1. See, for example, Mark Danner's extended essay, "The Truth of El Mozote," in *The New Yorker*, 6 December 1993.
2. For one account of the massacre, even if flawed by its anti-communist bias, see Thomas Anderson, *Matanza: El Salvador's 1932 Communist Revolt*, Lincoln, NE: University of Nebraska, 1971. Claribel Alegria and Darwin J. Flakoll's novel *Ashes of Izalco*, Willimantic CT: Curbstone Press, 1989, offers a powerful reconstruction of the events and aftermath of January 1932.

Part II   3 After the Fact: Ruth First and the Politics of Dissent in South Africa

1. See Barbara Harlow, *Barred: Women, Writing and Political Detention*, Hanover NH: Wesleyan University Press, 1992, Chapter 6.

2. Compare, for example, the title to the 1992 conference held in Cork, Ireland, "Where in the World is Ireland?"

3. Both Gillian Slovo and Shawn Slovo would reconstruct that narrative in works of their own – in *Ties of Blood*, Gillian Slovo's family saga extending over a century of generations, and Shawn Slovo's *A World Apart*, the screenplay and film that presents a renewed reading of mother/daughter relations affected by political detention.

Part III   New Geographies of Struggle

1. I have taken this formulation from Hilbourne A. Watson's essay, "Economic Globalization: NAFTA and its Consequences," in Phyllis Bennis and Michel Moushabeck, *Altered States: A Reader in the New World Order*, New York: Olive Branch Press, 1993. According to Watson, the "new geography of struggle demands new strategies of transformation to deal with the contradictions of capitalism at the regional and global level" (p. 136).

2. For an extended discussion of the "post-Oslo" period in Palestine/Israel, see Graham Usher, *Palestine in Crisis*, London: Pluto Press, 1995. Edward Said's critique of the agreement itself is particularly useful in its analysis of the historical compromises written into its text: see *Peace and its Discontents: Gaza Jericho 1993–1995*, London: Vintage, 1995.

Bibliography

Abrams, M. H. *Glossary of Literary Terms*. New York: Holt, Rinehart & Winston, 1981.

Abu-Jamal, Mumia. *Live from Death Row*. Reading MA: Addison-Wesley Publishing Company, 1995.

Adonis. "The Desert" in Mahmud Darwish, Samih al-Qasim, Adonis. *Victims of a Map*. Translated by Abdullah al-Udhari. London: Al-Saqi Books, 1984.

Alegría, Claribel and Flakoll, Darwin J. *Ashes of Izalco*. Willimantic CT: Curbstone Press, 1989.

Alpers, Edward A. and Fontaine, Pierre Michel. *Walter Rodney: Revolutionary and Scholar: A Tribute*. Los Angeles: Center for Afro-American and African Studies. UCLA, 1982.

Alvarado, Elvia. *Don't Be Afraid, Gringo: A Honduran Woman Speaks from the Heart*. Translated and edited by Medea Benjamin. San Francisco: Food First, 1987.

Americas Watch. *El Salvador's Decade of Terror: Human Rights Since the Assassination of Archbishop Romero*. New Haven and London: Yale University Press, 1991.

Anderson, Benedict. *Imagined Communities*. London and New York: Verso, 1991.

Anderson, Thomas. *Matanza: El Salvador's 1932 Communist Revolt*. Lincoln, NE: University of Nebraska, 1971.

Argueta, Manlio. *One Day of Life*. Translated by Bill Brow. New York: Random House, 1983.

Argueta, Manlio. *Cuzcatlan: Where the Southern Sea Beats*. Translated by Bill Brow. New York: Random House, 1987.

Ashcroft, Bill, Griffiths, Gareth and Tiffin, Helen. *The Empire Writes Back: Theory and Practice in Post-Colonial Literatures*. London and New York: Routledge, 1989.

Bernstein, Hilda. *The Rift: The Exile Experience of South Africans*. London: Jonathan Cape, 1994.

Beverley, John. "The margin at the center: On testimonio," *Modern Fiction Studies*, 35, 1, 1989.

Bindman, Geoffrey (Ed.). *South Africa: Human Rights and the Rule of Law*. London and New York: Pinter Publishers, 1988.

Boraine, Alex, Levy, Janet and Scheffer, Ronel (Eds). *Dealing with the Past: Truth and Reconciliation in South Africa*. Cape Town: Institute for Democracy in South Africa, 1994.

Breitman, George *et al. The Assassination of Malcolm X*. New York: Pathfinder Press, 1976.

Buntman, Fran. "Interview with Shawn Slovo" in *Cutting Through the Mountain*. Edited by Immanuel Suttner. South Africa: Penguin Books, forthcoming.

Cabral, Amilcar. *Unity and Struggle: Speeches and Writings*. Translated by Michael Wolfers. New York: Monthly Review Press, 1979.

Campbell, Brian, McKeown, Laurence and O'Hagan, Felim (Eds). *Nor Meekly Serve My Time: The H Block Struggle 1976–1981*. Belfast: Beyond the Pale Publications, 1994.

Carr, Matthew. "El Salvador: Birth of a New Culture," *Race and Class*, 36, 1, 1994.

Carson, Clayborn. *Malcolm X: The FBI File*. New York: Caroll & Graf Publishers, 1991.

Castañeda, Jorge. *Utopia Unarmed: The Latin American Left After the Cold War*. New York: Alfred Knopf, 1993.

Chabal, Patrick. *Amilcar Cabral: Revolutionary Leadership and People's War*. Cambridge: Cambridge University Press, 1983.

Christopher, A. J. *The Atlas of Apartheid*. New York and London: Routledge/ Johannesburg: Witwatersrand University Press, 1994.

Chungara, Domitila Barrios de. *Let Me Speak*. With Moema Vizzer. Translated by Victoria Ortiz. New York: Monthly Review Press, 1978.

Cohen, Stan. "Justice in Transition? Prospects for a

Palestinian–Israeli Truth Commission," *Middle East Report*, May–June/July–August 1995.

Comisión de la Verdad. *De la locura a la esperanza*. San José, Costa Rica: Editorial DEI, 1993.

Connell, Dan. "Palestine on the Edge: Crisis in the National Movement," *Middle East Report*, May–June/July–August 1995.

Cook, Allen. *South Africa: The Imprisoned Society*. London: International Defense and Aid Fund, 1974.

Darraj, Faysal. "The Current State of Arab Culture," *Democratic Palestine*, 33, June, 1989a.

Darraj, Faysal. "ll-Intifada: al-'ibda' al-siyasi wa-l-dhakira al-sha'biya" (The Intifada: Political Creativity and Popular Memory), *Al-Hadaf*, 962, 1989b.

Davidson, Basil. "On Revolutionary Nationalism: The Legacy of Cabral," *Race and Class*, 27, 3, 1986.

Davidson, Basil. *The Black Man's Burden: Africa and the Curse of the Nation State*. New York: Times Books, 1992.

Davis, Mike. "Who Killed Los Angeles? Part Two: The Verdict is Given," *New Left Review*, 189, 1993.

Debray, Régis. *Revolution in the Revolution? Armed Struggle and Political Struggle in Latin America*. Translated by Bobbye Ortiz. Harmondsworth: Penguin Books, 1968.

Debray, Régis. "Testimony at His Court Martial," in *The New Revolutionaries: A Handbook of the International Radical Left*. Edited by Tariq Ali. New York: William Morrow, 1969.

Debray, Régis. "Gracias, Roque . . .," *Estudios centroamericanos*, 331, May 1976.

Deutscher, Isaac. *The Prophet Outcast, Trotsky: 1929–1940*. Oxford and New York: Oxford University Press, 1963.

Dorfman, Ariel. *Death and the Maiden*. London: Nick Hern Books, 1991.

Dunkerley, James. *Political Suicide in Latin America and Other Essays*. New York and London: Verso, 1992.

Dunkerley, James. *The Pacification of Central America*. London and New York: Verso, 1994.

Eagleton, Terry. "Nationalism: Irony and Commitment" in Eagleton, Terry, Said, Edward and Jameson, Fredric. *Nationalism, Colonialism and Literature*. Minneapolis: University of Minnesota Press, 1990.

Farred, Grant. "Victorian with the Rebel Seed: C. L. R. James, Postcolonial Intellectual," *Social Text*, 38, 1994.

Ferguson, Douglas. "Walter Rodney's Application of Marxist Theory to the African Past and Present," in Alpers and Fontaine, 1982.

Ferro, Marc. "Entretien avec Marc Ferro," *Cahiers du cinéma*, 257, 1975.

Fontaine, Pierre Michel. "Walter Rodney: Revolutionary and Scholar in the Guyanese Political Cauldron," in Alpers and Fontaine, 1982.

Ford, Franklin. *Political Murder: From Tyrannicide to Terrorism*. Cambridge, MA: Harvard University Press, 1985.

Foster, Don, Davis, Dennis and Sandler, Diane. *Detention and Torture in South Africa: Psychological, Legal and Historical Studies*. New York: Saint Martin's Press, 1987.

Foucault, Michel. "Entretien avec Michel Foucault," *Cahiers du cinéma*, 251–252, 1974.

Foucault, Michel. "What Is an Author?" in Josue Harari (Ed.). *Textual Strategies*. Ithaca: Cornell University Press, 1979.

Galeano, Eduardo. "Quito, February 1976: I light the fire and beckon it," in Roque Dalton, *Poems*. Translated by Richard Schaaf. Willimantic, CT: Curbstone Press, 1984.

Galeano, Eduardo. "The Resurrections of Miguel Marmol," *Soberania*, 21, 1987.

Galeas, Geovani. *La conferencia y diálogos eternos*. Mexico: Correo Escénico/Artteatro, 1990.

Gordimer, Nadine. *A Guest of Honour*. New York: Viking, Penguin, 1983.

Gramsci, Antonio. "The Formation of the Intellectual," *Selections from the Prison Notebooks*. Edited and translated by Quintin Hoare and Geoffrey Nowell Smith. New York: International Publishers, 1983.

Grenier, Yvon. "Una clase política en transición," *Tendencias*, 14, October 1992.

Guha, Ranajit and Spivak, Gayatri Chakravorty. *Selected Subaltern Studies*. New York: Oxford University Press, 1988.

Hall, Stuart. *The Hard Road to Renewal*. London: Verso, 1988.

Hall, Stuart, *et al. Out of Apathy: Voices of the New Left 30*

Years On. London: Verso, 1989.

Harlow, Barbara. "Egyptian Intellectuals and the Debate on the 'Normalization' of Cultural Relations," *Cultural Critique*, 4, 1986.

Harlow, Barbara. *Resistance Literature*. London and New York: Methuen, 1987.

Harlow, Barbara. *Barred: Women, Writing and Political Detention*. Hanover NH: Wesleyan University Press, 1992.

Harvey, David. *The Condition of Postmodernity*. Cambridge, MA and Oxford: Blackwell, 1990.

Havens, M.C., Leiden, C. and Schmitt, M. K. *The Politics of Assassination*. New Jersey: Prentice-Hall, 1970.

Heath, Stephen. "Contexts," in *Questions of Cinema*. Bloomington: Indiana University Press, 1981.

Hector, Mario. *Death Row*. London: Zed Books, 1984.

Huberman, Leo and Sweezy, Paul (Eds). *Régis Debray and the Latin American Revolution*. New York: Monthly Review Press, 1969.

Hul, Qassim. *Al-sinima al-filastiniya (Palestinian Cinema)*. Beirut: Dar al-Auda, n.d.

Ince, Basil A. *Decolonization and Conflict in the United Nations: Guyana's Struggle for Independence*. Cambridge, MA: Schenkman Publishing Company, 1974.

James, C. L. R. "Walter Rodney and the Question of Power," in Alpers and Fontaine, 1982.

Johnson, Nels. *Islam and the Politics of Meaning in Palestinian Nationalism*. London: Kegan Paul International, 1982.

Kanafani, Anni. *Ghassan Kanafani*. Beirut: Near East Ecumenical Bureau, 1973.

Kasrils, Ronnie. *Armed and Dangerous: My Undercover Struggle Against Apartheid*. Oxford: Heinemann, 1993.

Kaufman, Natalie Hevener. *Human Rights Treaties and the Senate: A History of Opposition*. Chapel Hill and London: University of North Carolina Press, 1990.

Keck, Margaret E. "Typologies of Activism," *North American Congress on Latin America*, 28, 5, 1995.

Kelly, John D. "Diaspora and World War, Blood and Nation in Fiji and Hawaii," *Public Culture*, 7, 3, 1995.

Khalaf, Salah (Abou Iyad). *My Home, My Land*. With Eric

Rouleau. Translated by Linda Butler Koseoglu. New York: Times Books, 1981.

Khaled, Leila. *My People Shall Live*. Edited by George Hajjar. London: Hodder & Stoughton, 1973.

Kodesh, Wolfie. "Ruth First and New Age," *Sechaba*, September 1982.

Landsberg, Chris. "Isolation, Permanent Neutrality, Non-Alignment, or Internationalism: Towards a Post-Apartheid Foreign Policy Orientation," Johannesburg: Center for Policy Studies, International Relations series, 7, 1 February 1994.

Leys, Colin. "Africa's Tragedy," *New Left Review*, 204, 1994.

Linebaugh, Peter. "The Farce of the Death Penalty," *The Nation*, 14–21 August 1995.

Mafeje, Archie. "Soweto and its Aftermath," *Review of African Political Economy*, 11, January–April 1978.

Malcolm X. *Malcolm X: The Last Speeches*. Edited by Bruce Perry. New York: Pathfinder Press, 1989.

Mandela, Nelson. *No Easy Walk to Freedom*. Portsmouth: Heinemann, 1990.

Marquart, James W., Ekland-Olson, Sheldon and Sorensen, Jonathan R. *The Rope, the Chair, and the Needle: Capital Punishment in Texas 1923–1990*. Austin, TX: University of Texas Press, 1994.

Mattelart, Armand, Delcourt, X and Mattelart, M. *La culture contre la démocratie: L'audiovisuel a l'heure transnationale*. Paris: La découverte, 1984.

Mbeki, Govan. *South Africa: The Peasants' Revolt*. Harmondsworth: Penguin Books, 1964.

Mbeki, Govan. *Learning from Robben Island*. London: James Currey/Athens OH: Ohio University Press/Cape Town: David Philip, 1991.

Menchu, Rigoberta. *I. Rigoberta Menchu . . .* Edited by Elisabeth Burgos-Debray. Translated by Ann Wright. London: Verso, 1984.

Miah, Malik (Ed.). *The Assassination of Malcolm X*. New York, London and Sydney: Pathfinder Press, 1976.

Mixco, Miguel Huezo. "Muchachos: matad a Roque," *Diario Latino*, 29 August 1993.

Mofokeng, Zakes. *Never Again*. Performed at the University of Texas, Austin, 1 December 1995.

Moya, Horacio Castellanos. *La diáspora*. San Salvador: UCA Editores, 1989.

Moya, Horacio Castellanos. *Recuento de incertidumbres: Cultura y transición en El Salvador*. San Salvador: ediciones tendencias, 1993.

al-Naqib, Fadl. *Hakadha tantaha al-qusus hakadha tabda'a (Thus the stories end, thus they begin)*. Beirut: Institute for Arab Research, 1983.

Nixon, Rob. *Homelands, Harlem and Hollywood: South African Culture and the World Beyond*. New York and London: Routledge, 1994.

Nunca Más: The Report of the Argentine National Commission on the Disappeared. New York: Farrar Strauss Giroux (in association with *Index on Censorship*), 1984.

O'Connor, Frank. *The Lonely Voice*. Cleveland: World Publishing Co., 1963.

Odinga, Oginga. *Not Yet Uhuru*. New York: Mill and Wang, 1967.

Ondaatje, Michael. *The English Patient*. New York: Vintage International, 1993.

Perry, Bruce. *Malcolm X: The Life of a Man Who Changed Black America*. Barrytown, NY: Station Hill Press, 1991.

Petras, James and Morley, Morris. *Latin America in the Time of Cholera: Electoral Politics, Market Economics and Permanent Crisis*. New York and London: Routledge, 1992.

Pinnock, Don. *Ruth First and Radical South African Journalism in the 1950s*. Dissertation presented to Rhodes University, 1993.

Pinnock, Don. *Ruth First*. Johannesburg: Maskew Miller, 1995.

Podbrey, Pauline. *White Girl in Search of the Party*. Pietermaritzburg: Hadeda Books, 1993.

Report of the Chilean National Commission on Truth and Reconciliation (two volumes). Translated by Phillip E. Berryman. Notre Dame, IN: Center for Civil and Human Rights, Notre Dame Law School, 1993.

Rodney, Walter. *How Europe Underdeveloped Africa*. Washington DC: Howard University Press, 1974.

Rodney, Walter. *Walter Rodney Speaks: The Making of an African Intellectual.* Trenton, NJ: Africa World Press, 1990.

Romero, Archbishop Oscar. *Voice of the Voiceless: The Four Pastoral Letters and Other Statements.* Maryknoll, NY: Orbis Books, 1985.

Sachs, Albie. *The Jail Diary* (1966). London: Paladin Books, 1990a.

Sachs, Albie. "Preparing Ourselves for Freedom," in *Spring is Rebellious: Arguments about Cultural Freedom.* Edited by Ingrid de Kok and Karen Press. Cape Town: Buchu Books, 1990b.

Sachs, Albie. *The Soft Vengeance of a Freedom Fighter.* London: Grafton Books, 1990c.

Sachs, Albie. *Protecting Human Rights in the New South Africa.* Cape Town: Oxford University Press, 1990d.

Said, Edward W. "Introduction" to Halim Barakat. *Days of Dust.* Willmette, IL: Medina University Press International, 1974.

Said, Edward W. *The World, the Text, and the Critic.* Cambridge, MA: Harvard University Press, 1981.

Said, Edward W. *Peace and its Discontents: Gaza Jericho 1993–1995.* London: Vintage Books, 1995.

Salazar, General Leonardo A. Sanchez. *Murder in Mexico: The Assassination of Leon Trotsky.* With Julian Gorkin. Translated by Phyllis Hawley. Westport, CT: Hyperion Press, 1950.

Saro-Wiwa, Ken. *A Month and a Day: A Detention Diary.* Harmondsworth: Penguin Books, 1995.

Scott, Ann. "Interview," *Hecate,* 1980.

Scott, James. *Domination and the Arts of Resistance: Hidden Transcripts.* New Haven and London: Yale University Press, 1990.

Seabrook, Jeremy. *Victims of Development: Resistance and Alternatives.* London: Verso, 1993.

Segal, Ronald and First, Ruth (Eds). *South West Africa: Travesty of Trust.* London: André Deutsch, 1967.

Semprun, Jorge. "Preface" to Fernando Claudin. *The Communist Movement: from Comintern to Cominform* (vol. 1). Translated by Brian Pearce. New York and London: Monthly Review Press, 1975.

Slovo, Gillian. *Ties of Blood*. London: Michael Joseph, 1989.

Slovo, Joe. "Latin America and the Ideas of Régis Debray," *The African Communist*, 33, 1968.

Slovo, Joe. *Slovo: The Unfinished Autobiography*. With an introduction by Helena Dolny. Randberg: Ravan Press, 1995/London: Hodder & Stoughton, 1996.

Slovo, Shawn. *A World Apart*. London and Boston: Faber and Faber, 1988.

Slovo, Shawn. Interview with Fran Buntman (March 1995), for *Cutting Through the Mountain*.

Sobrino, Jon and Ellacuría, Ignacio. *Companions of Jesus: The Jesuit Martyrs of El Salvador*. Maryknoll, NY: Orbis Books, 1990.

Swedenburg, Ted. *Memories of Revolt: The 1936–39 Rebellion and the Palestinian National Past*. Minneapolis: University of Minnesota Press, 1995.

Thomas, Ewart. "Towards the Continuance of Walter Rodney's Work," in Alpers and Fontaine, 1982.

Tirado, Manlio. *La crisis política en El Salvador*. Mexico: Ediciones Quinto Sol, 1980.

Tomlinson, Mike. "Can Britain Leave Ireland? The Political Economy of War and Peace," *Race and Class*, 37, 1, 1995.

Torture in Brazil: A Report by the Archdiocese of São Paulo. Translated by Jaime Wright. Edited by Joan Dassin. New York: Vintage Books, 1986.

Turki, Fawaz. "To Be a Palestinian," *Journal of Palestine Studies*, 3, 3, 1974.

Turki, Fawaz. *Soul in Exile: Lives of a Palestinian Revolutionary*. New York: Monthly Review Press, 1988.

Uruguay: Nunca Más: Human Rights Violations, 1972–1985. Translated by Elizabeth Hampsten. Philadelphia: Temple University Press, 1992.

Usher, Graham. *Palestine in Crisis*. London: Pluto Press, 1995.

Villalobos, Joaquín. *Una revolución en la izquierda para una revolución democrática*. San Salvador: Arcoiris, 1992.

Watson, Hilbourne A. "Economic Globalization: NAFTA and its Consequences," in Bennis, Phyllis and Moushabeck, Michel.

Altered States: A Reader in the New World Order. New York: Olive Branch Press, 1993.

Weinglass, Leonard. *Race for Justice: Mumia Abu-Jamal's Fight Against the Death Penalty*. Monroe ME: Common Courage Press, 1995.

White, Hayden. "The Politics of Historical Interpretation," *Critical Inquiry*, 9, 1982.

Whitfield, Teresa. *Paying the Price: Ignacio Ellacuría and the Murdered Jesuits of El Salvador*. Philadelphia: Temple University Press, 1995.

Wilkinson, Tracy. "Requiem for a Betrayed Poet," *Los Angeles Times*, 9 August 1994.

Williams, Brackette A. *Stains on My Name, War in My Veins: Guyana and the Politics of Cultural Struggle*. Durham and London: Duke University Press, 1991.

Wolpe, AnnMarie. *The Long Way Home*. London: Virago Press, 1994.

Woods, Donald. *Biko*. New York: Henry Holt and Company, 1987.